CLOSE
TO MY
HEART

YoungWriters

First published in Great Britain by Young Writers in 2003
Young Writers, Remus House, Coltsfoot Drive,
Peterborough PE2 9JX
Tel: 01733 890066

SB ISBN 1 84460 236 2

Foreword

The following poems were all drawn from the cream of an extremely impressive selection of work. They were written by a broad range of eleven to sixteen-year-olds for our 2003 *Close To My Heart* competition.

The overall standard was high, with entrants interpreting the *Close To My Heart* theme in a range of interesting and often surprisingly imaginative ways. The poems included reflect this, with poems on a diverse range of themes, ranging from the value of friendship and family members to favourite football teams, role models and pop stars.

Ultimately, we hope that above all else, *Close To My Heart* proves a hugely entertaining read. Whether funny, powerful, moving, eccentric or sad, we hope you enjoy reading these poems as much as we enjoyed choosing them.

Contents

Wild And Enchanting

A herd of horses in the sunset dance
With shiny chestnut coats and golden flecks
All diving, lively, sprightly is their stance
With glossy summer manes against their necks
The horses all alert, their ears a-prick
As danger lurks around the corner near
The frightened mares and foals together stick
All through the herd there is a sense of fear.
Amongst the grass the horses do lie still
These horses work united as a team
Once more the mood returns calm and tranquil
The sun again breaks through the clouds and beams
And once again a fresh new day does dawn
And with it, hope and love will greet the morn.

A sonnet by Imogen Bexfield (11)

1st Prize

LEXIBOOK **LEXIBOOK Tablet 108 With Simcard Reader**
This handy PDA enables you to; read, copy and write to
mobile phone Simcards and is fully synchronised with
Microsoft Windows 95, 98, 2000, NT, XP & Outlook. It also
comes complete with a PC link kit that allows you to
download digital books from the Internet.

My Song

I hear the song, the song that sings
A hundred thousand crazy things.
The summer days laughing with friends
The summer nights that had no end.
The times we had, I'll never lose
Hazy madness, dancing shoes,
The soundtrack to our finest hour
Hearing those notes has a spellbinding power.
A power to make my heart skip a beat
The lyrics to make me sing in the street
I sing of love and happiness
Who could ask for more or less?
But the thing I care for most of all
Was the day I stood up proud and tall
The heat and the sweat were egging me on
On the day that was known for that wonderful song
I'd never known such exhilaration or glee
Than when you sang that song with me.

Ria Farrell (14)

Runner-up

Too Good To Be True

When you left
My tears fell like rain
Forming seas and rivers of pain.
The skies went dark
And I watched clouds appear
They filled my heart with
Hate and fear.
I loved you once
A long time ago
I'd been foolish
Now I know.
I should have seen it in your eyes
But my mind was plagued
With all your lies.
When I kissed you, I should have tasted
The flavour of deceit
And time been wasted.
I didn't want to believe it
But I always knew
No matter who says it
Love's too good to be true.

Sarah Willingham (14)

Runner-up

Not Even A Shadow

The news stole the place of after school chat.
Broke the daily chain with a sharp chisel,
Driven into me.

Familiar air became heavy, rife with it.
Images spurted from Mum's account.
She saw his little lean body convulsing beyond his control.

His little lean body lying there.
Motionless in a cardboard box.
Instantly taken from life and from us.

Wrapped in a blanket that couldn't warm him.
Placed in the ground as cold as his body had become.
An alien place for him to lie.

Trying too hard to be a good mourner,
Fragments of useless thoughts poured in,
Dimming my perfect memory.

His friends poked their heads through the gate and knew.
They sat quietly by his grave under the tree.

Don't pile on the clichés, don't say, 'He was *only* ...'
I should glance across and see him dreaming on the chair,
I should hear his call at the door, asking in.

Not even a shadow
To materialise my memory, all that I have.

Rebecca Riddles (16)

Runner-up

Close To My Heart

A laugh,
A look,
The echo of a sound.
A movement,
A phrase,
Trails me like a hound.
A smile given carelessly,
Treasured, kept.
Gone away for a year and a day,
To return, it is hoped.
If not,
Then I'll live with the knowledge
That fate and chance
Hold happiness locked in a room.

Alicia Williams (15)

Close To My Heart

What's close to my heart are the ones that I've lost,
They keep me safe through the wind and the frost.

Although I miss them every day,
I should not cry with dismay.

Because they've not gone away from me,
They're still inside, where they always will be.

And as I look up to the sky at night,
There's someone there, making sure I'm alright.

My guardian angels in the stars,
Where they will stay, forever close to my heart.

Jenny Langskog (12)

My Mother

My steady rock, in a stormy sea,
My beautiful rose, in a garden of weeds,
My radiant sun, in a cloudy sky,
My tiny glimmer, in the corner of my eye.
My wonderful angel, with a heart of gold,
My piece of silk, with delicate folds,
My hand, to wipe away glistening tears,
My barrier, to keep away all my fears.

My mother, for whom my love never ends,
Forever and ever, we will always be friends.

Catherine Barnes (13)

In Loving Memory Of Tom

Do not weep,
Do not cry,
For I am here in your mind -
For I am here.
I will never leave you until you die
For I am the stars that light up your sky.

Hal Phillips (11)

The Closest Things To My Heart

The third closest thing to my heart
Is my backbone
It gives my life structure
It helps me experience new feelings
And it always lifts me up when I'm down
Without my backbone,
I don't think I could even stand up in the morning

The second closest things to my heart
Are my lungs
They take my breath away
(About 1440 times a day)
They make me hold my breath when I think of them
I just can't get them out of my system
In fact, I don't think I could live without them

Overall, my heart's best friend is blood
Blood keeps me going throughout the day
I love it so much, it makes me blush
It helps give me an adrenaline rush
When I cut myself
Blood is the first thing there to help me
Without my blood, lungs and backbone, I'd feel non-existent.

Ruth Beattie (12)

Good Day Special Friend

When clouds call down with anger,
Threatening to enclose my life in darkness
My special friend wanders by
And gives a friendly smile.

My feelings have been crushed
Like lumps of dry dirt,
He wanders into my mind
And cures my crushing.

So when my feelings are crushed
And clouds call down with anger
I see Jack and remember,
He shares his happiness with me.

As my final dedication verse,
On the outside he is a dog,
Inside is my special friend.

Good day special friend.

Jessica Beaver (13)

Fallen In Love

F allen for you all over again
A ll I'll ever want or need for the rest of my life
L ove is in the air when you come near
L ocked in your arms because you make me feel safe
E ager to meet you whenever I can
N aughty to sneak out and meet you in the middle of the night

I n your heart for the rest of my life and for evermore
N ear you every second of every day forever

L ove so strong that it can never be broken, not ever
O pen feelings, secrets, truth is what love is
V ows that can never be broken and happiness forever and a day
E very moment of every day you're in my mind.

Gemma Wood (15)

Ode To My Boyfriend

Each time I catch a glimpse,
My heart skips a beat,
I intake a sharp breath,
My hands begin to heat.

He is so special to me,
An angel in my dark world,
The only one who stops me,
When into despair I am hurled.

He is the sweetest guy I know,
He treats me like I'm real,
He is the only one for me,
I hope our love is sealed.

He has stood by me through
Thick and through thin,
He must be my hero,
I owe so much to him.

I wish I could express,
The feelings in my heart,
To my wonderful boyfriend,
Even if just a part.

Joanne Mcentee (15)

Papa

He can't be with me all the time
And that I do hate.
But it makes the times we have together,
Precious, special and great.

He can't be with me all the time
And, sure, it makes me glum
And occasionally, just sometimes,
It feels like I'm missing out on fun.

He can't be with me all the time
And although we've had to part,
He is my papa, my father
And will always be close to my heart.

Marina Leoni (13)

Family Forever

Everyone has something
That they love and treasure
Mine are my family
I'll love them forever.

Never yet have I been wrong
About who are the greatest
I choose my family
They keep me on my toes then give me time to rest.

They treat you as equals
And give you respect
If there was a vote to see who are the best
I'd choose my family - that's who I'd elect
- Yes, that's who I'd elect.

Anna Senkiw (12)

Friends Forever

I've got lots of friends,
Five of them are special,
Frankie, Emma, Clare, Jess and Hannah.

Emma has been a lifelong friend,
I hope our friendship will never end.

Hannah knows my ways,
We can talk about nothing for days.

Then there is Clare,
When you need her she is always there.

Jess is the person for advice, so I ring,
We talk about the troubles life can bring.

Frankie and I have a special bond which is clear to see,
Few are as close as Frankie and me.

This poem officially states
These are the greatest *ever* mates!

Georgie Field (11)

A Mother's Alphabet

A is for amazing, my mother is just that.
B is for bonkers, and
C razy you see.
D is for the dreams she helps me fulfil.
E is for exciting, we have so much
F un together.
G is for great, she's the greatest in the world.
H is for happy, the way she makes me feel.
I is for interest, she helps me with my work.
J is for jewel, she's as precious as can be.
K is the kind and
L oving person that she is.
M is for Mum, this poem is for her.
N is for near - she's never far away.
O is for the outings she always takes me on.
P is for Princess, her special name for me.
Q is for Queen, we're as close as can be.
R is for really, really
S pecial to me.
T is for tease, I tease my mum so much.
U is for utterly awesome, she's the top of her class.
V is for the variety of things she always does for me.
W is for the wonderful wife she is to my dad.
X xx, the kisses she plants on my cheeks.
Y is for yack - she loves talking on the phone, and
Z is for the zillions of things she sacrifices
   to give me the very best experiences.

Thank you Mum, you're the best in the world!

Jessica Vickery (13)

Thank You

Thank you Lord for the wonderful Earth,
Thank you for the mothers, who gave birth,
What would the world be without light?
What would the world do without night?

Think of a world without any flowers
Where would we be without any power?
Think about a world without any leaves
What would happen to the lovely breeze?

We thank you for life to live
And all we have to do is give.
Some people do all the taking,
When others help with the entire making.

Some people can't appreciate the world and people,
What if it was them that had to sacrifice their family's lives?
Thank you for the school we learn in
What have we done to deserve such beautiful places to be in?

This is why we all have duties,
To take special care of our community.

Stephanie Smith (13)

Friends

F riends are cool and caring
R enting vids are scaring
I   mmature, so young and free
E ating all we like, that's me!
N ot caring about a thing, just
D aring, sharing, having a laugh, that's what a friend …
S hould do! And be!

Stacey-Jane Viney (13)

Hull City Are The Best In The World

Time ticked, Tigers kicked
Bournemouth bashed, ref crashed
Crowd roared, ball soared
Hit bar, Hull hurrah!

Bournemouth came, score became
Away one, home none.

Whittle whacked
The ball was smacked
Walters rushed, stadium hushed
Scored a goal

Hull glad, Bournemouth sad

Hull 2, Bournemouth 1
Elliot scored, fans roared

Second half scorer Elliot
In the net, did anyone bet
Final score, a win to Hull
With Bournemouth looking very dull.

Harry Holmes (11)

Special To Me

My bedroom's my most special thing
Better than a TV or a ring
It's the place where I chill out and relax
My radio is turned up to 'max'.
My bedroom contains all the things I own -
My bed, radio, my mobile phone (and more)
My bedroom is decorated lilac and pink,
The best colours ever . . . well, I think.
Inside my bedroom I have a TV
And a DVD player, and loads of DVDs.
My bedroom is always full of noise
And full of loads of cuddly toys.
My bedroom is great,
So special to me
I just need a sign saying . . .
Sisters - no entry!

Vicki Jones (13)

Friendship

Someone to rely on
Someone to care for
Someone to love
Someone to hate
Someone so special

Someone to share happiness with
Someone to share sadness with
Someone to celebrate with
Someone to go out with
Someone so special

Someone to argue with
Someone to comfort
Someone to share special moments with
Someone to drink coffee with
Someone so special

Someone to talk to
Someone to lend a helping hand
Someone to listen to
Someone that means so much to you
Someone so special.

Samantha Dorrington (13)

My Family

My family is so special, no one could disagree,
My mum and brother, cousins and more, oh and not forgetting me.
Starting with my mum, who I could never live without,
Even if she tells me off and almost always shouts.

Second we have my brother, who I've loved from the start,
Sometimes we have our differences but I love him with all my heart.
Then we have my cousins who are the maddest you can get,
But I would never swap them for anyone I've ever met.

Now we have my uncles and grandads, who are really, really funny
And I love them even though they give me lots of money.
Next we have my nans and aunties who spend and shop like mad,
But even if they had no money, they're the best I've ever had.

Now you know my family, not forgetting my cat,
So let's see if you can find a better family than that!

Alicia Gleeson (12)

A Girl's Best Friend

(In memory of Roxie)

We grew up for years together,
I thought you would be here forever,
But now I know you had to go,
I hope you know I loved you so,
I never got to say goodbye,
For I never knew that you would die,
Even now, I still miss you
And I hope that you miss me too,
You're still in my mind and even my heart,
I really wish we were never apart
And the saddest thing that makes me cry,
Is that I never said . . . *goodbye!*

Lauren Johnson (13)

I Will Remember . . .

You left me several years ago,
Through no real fault of your own.
I miss you so much that my heart breaks each day,
But the gift you bestowed takes some of the heartache away.

The locket is hung carefully around my neck,
I like to draw comfort from the sheer weight of it.
It must be the most valuable thing that I own,
Especially as it's something you once gave a home.

Our pictures are inside, your eyes shining bright,
I gaze at it silently, each day and each night.
Never again will we laugh, dance and play,
No more bedtime hugs, my nightmares will stay.

But I feel like your soul is locked in its case.
My heart-shaped golden locket,
My mother's last trace.

Emma Kosminsky (14)

Close To My Heart She Ran

There was something,
Something very ...
Weird!
It was an Earthling,
The same as one of me,
It spoke in manor, respect and in a normal tone,
It said, 'Come here my little sunshine,'
So ...
I ran ...
And ran ...
But I got nowhere,
So ...
Everything went black,
Pitch-black to be more precise,
Well ... actually to be even more precise ...
Silence!
Then my dog opened his mouth,
And said ...
'You're not going to go anywhere at this rate ...
You need to start loving,
Caring,
And stop talking to yourself!'
Everything went back,
'Well aren't you coming?'
So I just sat there, my eyes started leaking,
And said ...
'I love yo ... yo ... you!'

Hamzah Ghaleb (13)

Remember

Have you ever looked into the night
And seen the stars shining bright?
The golden, glistening white
I stare with all my might
Remembering the sight
Of the beckoning stars at night.

They seem to shine so bright
The silver, sparkling white
I watch with all my might
Never forgetting the sight
Of the fascinating stars at night.

They always shine so bright
The sparkle of the white
I glare with all my might
Gazing at the sight
That only occurs at night.

Sylvia Fraser (13)

Friends

Friends, you can never have enough
But they come in different groups
Best, good and not so good
But why?

Friends also cause trouble
Jealousy and selfishness, come to the top of my head
What's the point of having friends
If all they do is hurt you?

But they do come in handy,
When you get into trouble,
Or when you need them for support,
But is it worth it?

If friends hurt you, never go back,
They'll only hurt you some more,
They'll back chat
And you never know if they're true friends.

So in conclusion you have to trust them,
If they're good they'll be with you through anything,
If they're bad, well you have to find that out for yourself,
So all you have to do for the moment is trust them!

Lesha Nair (12)

Future Express

When the flag goes down and my train pulls out,
Onto the open rails,
My one-way ticket,
For a lifetime's journey.
I'll look over my shoulder and smile.
Dark forests loom up ahead,
I don't know what they hold,
It's all uphill for quite a way,
But I'll look back and remember,
Birthdays, Easter, Christmas and school
Infants, juniors, Queen Anne's and Canonlee.
I'll look to the future with my memories intact,
It's my box of chocolates, each a different favourite,
All mine, all mine, I keep adding to my collection,
Where am I going,
What will I do,
Who will I meet,
Will I see you.
I'm like a blind man,
Who can't stop moving,
Nothing lasts forever, it all has to change,
I have my head held high,
Flash my smile, grit my teeth and ...
Full steam ahead, to life as I'll soon know it,
Leave behind what I already know,
Don't worry, we'll all remember,
Our fun times, mad jokes,
And like the drama crazed thespian that I am,
I'd just like to say ... I won't just remember,
I'll be back.

Dominé Wright (16)

From Daughter To Mother

(Dedicated to Jill Bradley - my mum)

Mum, it's that time again,
A time to celebrate,
How good you are at stopping me,
From making you go insane!

You're such a caring mother, anyone can see,
You're here, there and everywhere,
But you'll always be there for me.

There's been our good moments,
Our bad moments.
You've shouted, I've shouted,
But it's all worth it in the end,
As that friendship we break will always mend.

And that friendship we break is priceless to me,
Wouldn't sell it for the world.
You're my mum, I love you, couldn't live without you.
And when I look into your eyes,
A heart of gold I see.

Mum, you're my heart, soul and life,
I can't express how much you mean to me.
And in life, if I turn out to be half the person you are,
I will have achieved something.

And remember,
I will love you forever.

Megan Bradley (12)

Footie Nights

Come on England, we need to win,
They are winning so let's all sing.
England are the best team in the world,
Owen shoots and it curled.
Footie days floating away but ah, oh those footie nights,
A goal, a goal, a goal, a goal.

Tell me more, tell me more did he score any goals?
Tell me more, tell me more what about Paul Scholes?
Aha, aha, aha, aha goal!

Was it Beckham, was it Scholes who scored our winning goals?
As the crowd cheers and cheers
Out of nowhere Heskey appears
Footie sun, it has begun, but ah, oh those footie nights.
A goal, a goal, a goal, a goal.

Tell me more, tell me more who can score?
Tell me more, tell me more did he score anymore?

Jessica Houlden (12)

Close To My Heart: You're My Song, Mom

(This is for my mom)

Are you an angel from above,
Because you're always full of love?
The universe is not worth as much,
As your warm and gentle touch.

You are so beautiful and full of wisdom,
Keep me from wrong and show me the true meaning of freedom,
You have taught me to do right
And only for my dignity to fight.

When I give up and cry,
You encourage me to try,
You take away my frown,
Whenever I am feeling down.

You let me stand tall alone,
But when I fall you bring me home,
There is no one who can take your place,
I love you from here and to beyond space.

I admire when you face pain,
You beat it away with a cane
And when you have no money
You say, 'It doesn't matter honey.'

I hope your life is happy and long
And I pray each step you make is never wrong,
Mom you are so brave and strong,
I want you to know, you're my song.

Rupinder 'Rozz' Phangura

Close To My Heart

How awful this day is
Without you here.
A shining star, a bright light.
It's gone.

The house seems grey and sombre,
Outside the winds hear my cries
For the little but major part in my life.
My tabby cat.

No one pit-a-patting,
No one disturbing me for food,
No fluffy animal
Who's barely awake all day.

The armchair empty, though
Her fluff still lives on.
Our only remembrance of her.
Today is so long.

As I look out into the darkening world,
A pair of bright, glimmering eyes shine,
The moon glimmers on her waddling body
As she pit-a-pats back home.

In comes Violet,
Sad-faced and soaked.
The most adorable cat in the world.
My flower's back and she's mine.

Rachel Moloney (11)

Close To My Heart

As a salty tear falls down my flushed cheeks,
It's support and comfort that I seek.
No one understands me, I need someone to hold
And who happens to come in from the cold?

I sigh a breath of relief as he strolls to see me.
To my strained heart, he holds the key.
A smile slowly creeps across my face,
As he comes to sit with me with elegance and grace.

He stares intently with his beautiful green eyes,
I soon forget about all the deceitfulness and lies.
He can tell that something isn't quite right,
As I hold him close to my heart so tight.

My body feels lighter, as he starts to heal my heart.
In the story of my life he plays a unique and special part.
The sensation of holding someone I love so much
Is so strong that I feel better with every single touch.

His purr brings joy and happiness to my ears,
His presence and comfort stops my flow of tears.
He seems to lift me sky-high and my mind reassures
With his smooth, soft coat and gentle padding paws.

My heart feels lighter, as reality sinks in.
What had really made me feel better was having him
Close to my heart always and forever.
He is so special to me, I will forget him never.

Cassie Emanuel (14)

My Cat Sam

My cat Sam is very old
He's even older than me
I can't believe I have a pet
That was born before me.

My cat Sam is very old
His faded ginger fur
Looks old and tired
And his sharp green eyes
Look sad and lonely.

My cat Sam is very old
He sleeps all day
On the sofa next to my mom
On the floor next to the door
He even sleeps among the twigs
And leaves in the garden.

My cat Sam is very old
He's like a bag of bones
But most of all
My cat Sam means
The whole wide world to me.

Sophie Baker (13)

Memories

My tottering legs, unsure of their direction,
followed the wooden push-cart along the floor.

My eager hands held the ice cream in front of my waiting mouth.
It was my first ice cream with milk in it. A discovery for my tongue.

My happy face watching a friend. A friend I hold dear
in my heart even after her passing away.

My nervous mind on a first day of school.
It was soon going to calm.

My torn excitement and distress when leaving my family
and embarking on school trips.

My slow tear, trickling down my face
when I learnt of my parents' separation.

My bursting anger
when my family is hurt in any way.

My emphatic joy when I have the knowledge
that I have helped somebody.

My aching longing when having to leave
someone or something behind.

My eager happiness that I have
experienced all through my life.

My memories, without which I would know nothing
about myself and be no one.

Nadia Anaïs Bowyer (15)

Heaven

Heaven is another world
Life in Heaven is like a dream
Heaven is full of peace and happiness
With laughter all around

Many people live in Heaven
And look down on us with loving eyes
You and me will be there some day
Looking down with our angel eyes
Watching out for our loved ones left behind
Waiting to welcome them home.

Kaylie Conner (14)

Irreplaceable

You are irreplaceable.
There is no one like you
And there never will be
Ever.

No one will ever be as brave as you
As strong as you
As determined as you.

No one will ever laugh like you
Ever smile like you
Ever joke like you.

No one can ever be like you
Because you are
Irreplaceable.

Sarah Sheppard

Parents Care!

Mum and Dad are always there
They help you in many different ways!
Parents really care for you,
24/7 - all the hours in the day.

They give you a hug and hold you close.
Protect you from all the hateful things,
When you tell them you love them the most.
Keeping you warm, loved and very safe!

When they get cross and tell you off,
They're not showing you who is boss.
They do it because they care!
Even when you whine and pout,
Telling them, 'It's not fair!'

Parents love you for who you are.
To them it doesn't matter, you're their little star!
Parents love you for what you are,
If you came to harm, it'd break their hearts.
You're very special to them ... yes you are!

Sarah Bromberg (14)

My Nan

My nan can be fun
Though she's very old
She can be quite annoying
But to me she's better than gold

My nan found last year hard
Because my grandad died
But this year she tries to be better
And never normally cries

My nan is always kind
Unless I'm very bad
Sometimes she even pretends
To be very hippy and mad

My nan can forget things
From time to time
Another thing she loves is jelly
Her favourite flavour is lime

My nan is a little deaf
So she cannot hear very well
So when someone is at the door
She says, 'Was that the bell?'

Sarah Mellers (11)

Friendship

My best friend's a brilliant mate
We met through simple fate
A smile across a crowded room
Lifted spirits, forgotten gloom
A bond was made and never broken
Though not a word had been spoken
And now nothing can tear us apart
Inseparable from the start
'Til the break of dawn we talk and chat
'Bout silly things like purple cats
I know she'll always be there
In times of sadness and scares
We'll take on the world together
And our friendship will last forever.

Laura Fergusson

Sending Love

I'll send it by postcard
With a first class stamp,
I'll send it by car
With the boot full of kisses,
I'll send it by plane
With it bursting with hugs,
I'll send it by water
With the sea full of roses,
I'll send it by balloon,
Let it sail through your heart,
However it gets there
Whenever it gets there
You'll be sure to be struck by Cupid.

Kayleigh Fuller (13)

The Closest Thing To My Heart

There is one thing in this world that is closest to my heart,
And I never ever want us to be apart.
It is not money or a material thing,
It's not TV, music or even a diamond ring.
It comes from your family and even your closest friends,
It comes from deep down and it never ever ends.
Sometimes you find it hard to forget and forgive,
But without this thing I just couldn't live.
It's sometimes hard to give it, and you can't always show it,
But you could always write a poem even if you're not a poet.
The thing I am talking about is sent from above,
This thing, this gift is love.

Rachael Mellers (13)

My Best Friend

You are not only there to listen
But also there to understand
Whenever I am feeling sad and blue
You always find a way to cheer me up
Just thinking about you puts a smile on my face
I can tell you anything
'Cause I know my secrets are safe with you
You are always there for me
In good times and in bad times
We have shared so many wonderful times together
And I know there are more to come, till the end of time
You are my best buddy
And I am thankful to you
I will cherish you forever and keep you close to my heart
Because I found a true best friend in you and I love you!

Agnes Birunji (15)

Grandad

The way he sat in the chair looking puzzled by the crossword.
The way he fell asleep in the kitchen whilst watching Countdown.
The way he took me in his arms and cuddled me when I was scared.
The love I felt for him so strong, please let it last forever.

We went to the park on a regular basis.
He'd push me high on the swings and I'd roar with laughter.
If I fell he caught me, if I hurt my knee he'd rub it better!
The love I felt for him so strong, please let it last forever.

He read me books and then I read to him.
The hours we spent together; so much fun.
The things he taught me so wise and useful.
The love I felt for him so strong, please let it last forever.

The cards I made for his birthday, childish and uneven.
He didn't care, all the more treasured they were,
The love I felt for him so strong, please let it last forever.

The months and years went by so quickly.
The time came when I could do the crossword!
The less I saw of my dear old grandad.
The love I felt for him so strong, please let it last forever.

The day came when the phone rang and Dad's face drained of colour.
Grandad was ill in hospital, the guilt I felt for not seeing him so often.
The love I felt for him so strong, please let it last forever.

The funeral came and went and I visited his grave.
The home-made cards found in drawers.
The sadness felt by one and all.
The love I felt for him so much stronger.

I live with the thoughts of my grandad,
All the good times we shared stored in my mind.
The love I feel for him so strong and it will last forever.

Kelly James (16)

Love

I thank God, He sent you to me,
For you and I were meant to be,
When I see you my heart skips a beat,
You make my whole life complete.

We have a bond too strong to break,
We have a love no one can take,
I love your eyes, soul, body and mind,
A love like ours is hard to find.

You alone are my one desire,
Just one kiss sets my heart on fire.

Sam Poulson (11)

School

A baby I was when I came here
Dropping out my eye was more than one tear
Working wasn't my thing
But all I wanted to do was to sing
Boy did I hope it didn't rain
So everyone would be in pain
See we all wanted to play
We went into lunch
Boy, would you see me munch
School life got fun
'Cause we had more of the sun
And now I stand here to say goodbye
To teachers and all
But before that I want to say
To teachers and all
Their education is cool
The brain is the best tool
So I want to finish off
And say Lodge Farm is the best school!

Naila Yaqub (12)

Goodbye Grandad

It was a bright, sunny February day
When the clock ran out it was time to say,
Goodbye to you with all our hearts
Memories never fade, we'll never part.

Your stories you told never failed to impress
Your help with others showed us your great kindness,
The matches you saw, made you so proud
Whether wet, hot or cold you were there in the crowd.

Your face with that smile and that short grey hair
We were happy to see you whenever you were there,
The cards you sent will be kept close to us
On our birthdays you always caused a fuss.

Your memory lives on with Harry your dog
Who sleeps by your chair like a wooden log,
So I bid you farewell and ask you this; will we forget you?
Never. Rest in peace, forever and ever.

Sam Lancaster (14)

Family Memories

Enclosed within my tranquil heart,
My closest memories can't depart.
My family behind me all the way,
The past, the future and the present day.
The more than adequate memory for me
Will stay with me forever, pure love is the key.

Initially I thought only I could succeed,
Dependency followed, family I need.
The memories I have of my family and I
Are priceless, and that's what money can't buy.
The more than adequate memory for me
Will stay with me forever, pure love is the key.

Unfortunate people can't share that true feeling.
There's a space in their heart which needs desperate healing.
People need to share more devotion,
Show some support put the hope wheels in motion.
The more than adequate memory for me
I would share with more people, pure love is the key.

Sarah Gardner (14)

It's Raining In Me, But She Can See?

It's raining outside, it's raining in me
Two green eyes stare up and see
She jumps upon my lap, she's so sweet
Tabs and I our cuddles meet

My brother and I have just had a fight
But Tabitha cared, I knew she might
First one paw upon each shoulder
Now look, she is becoming bolder

Cheek against cheek she nuzzles my face
When I'm with her I forget this place
Then her rough tongue against my chin
My family look at me as if it's a sin

My cat jumps off as I'm called for tea
Her sleek, black fur shimmers at me
Softly Tabitha claws at my leg
And looks at her food bowl which is empty instead

A thankful miaow, I give her her food
My family at dinner seems subdued
Tabitha comes to brighten the scene
But no one except me seems very keen

Eventually I have to say goodnight
I have to keep Tabitha out of sight
Because if she knew I was going to bed
She would follow me with eyes that said 'stay instead'.

Charlotte Spinney (11)

Lily

You often hear comments about Lily
About how she would have loved things
She was desperate for my parents to have a child
And when I came she was overjoyed.
I remember how she was always at family gatherings
It's a tradition we all keep.
When I think back I realise I don't remember much
I wish I could but I can't
Every now and again I hear a story and keep it stored in place
I know that she was my great, great aunty
She was my grandad's aunt.
I know little about her but I know this
She loved my mum, my dad and me
Everything my dad did she was proud of
Anything new and exciting
Everyone would have known about it.
She would have told her friends, and the ladies in the library.
So even though I don't know much,
I know enough.
I know that Lily Green was a wonderful lady
Who loved me, and my family
Someone who will never be forgotten
And always loved.

Emma Paulus (13)

Our Love

I am deeply submerged in a red sea of love,
Sometimes it is like I am drowning. Drowning and floundering,
But I can get no oxygen. I cannot have love and live at the same time.
It is as if the sun only rises because you are there,
And the only thing that keeps me alive is you and my love for you.
But it is not the same for you.
My adoration was cast aside,
My devotion humiliated.
And all that is left of me is an empty shell with you inside.
For I am forever trapped within the confines of your love.
I cannot move, breathe or feel without you entering my troubled mind.
From a love so pure has sprung a hate so cold.
I cannot move. You are close to my heart, but it has turned to stone.
I cannot get you out of my life. You sit nestled,
And embroidered like an unwanted thread in my heart,
And everyday a stitch breaks and another part of me dies
With the remaining thoughts of you.
Our love was a passionate one, that burned and consumed
And now there is nothing left except you.

Ashley Fryer (14)

Old Best Friends

We've been friends for 9 years
We've seen each other shed a lot of tears

We've spoken about all of our fears
Those were the best years

Now it feels like we have grown apart
We'll never be in each other's hearts

All the time we seem to fight
It feels like I can't do anything right

I still wish we could be close friends
But now we are just old best friends.

Alicia Thompson (13)

Treacle My Black Cat

Treacle, Treacle my tiny black cat
I'll give you some tuna, if you come back
Your fur was soft and warm
Your nose like a velvety ice cube
Please, please will you come back?
Treacle, my little black cat
Eyes would widen, ready for the pounce
With your collar bells ringing, you made a lot of noise
Oh, why, why did you have to go?
You used to climb the curtains,
Swinging to and fro.
I miss you, if only you knew how much.
You were the smallest in the litter,
That's why we chose you.
Treacle, Treacle my tiny black cat.

Hayley Sherlock (11)

Waiting

I waited,
But you never came.
I questioned,
But you never answered.
I gave you my heart,
But you threw it away with scorn.
I loved,
But you never loved back.
I gave,
But you never gave in return.
I cried out,
But you never listened.
I prayed,
But you never answered my prayers.
I slaved,
But you never lifted a finger.
I sobbed,
But you never came to dry my tears.

I waited,
But you never came.

Sally Clayton (12)

Close To My Heart

C lose to my heart I hold my friend
L ooking deep into her brown eyes, I see
O bvious friendship with patience and care
S troking her soft black hair
E ven though she speaks not in my tongue

T he bond that has formed holds strong
O f all my friends she'll never leave not even in death

M y heart shall not part from her, a bond of friendship
Y ou'll never understand until the day you have lost it

H earts are stubborn and kind, I know only of this friendship
E ven I do not fully understand
A nd no one ever shall, I bet you're thinking I'm a boy
R everse that thought, no I'm not a boy
T he friendship I share is not human at all
   but my young Border collie called Susy.

Samantha Livingston (13)

Close To My Heart

People have many things close to them,
But no one has anyone as close to them as my friends,
Morning, break time, lunch and after school,
Us friends are together acting cool,
Whenever we have some spare time,
Us mates are talking about our lives,
Tantrums, bad moods, silly fights and laziness,
We're told they are the symptoms of being a teenager,
We no way think we are at all like this,
But our parents say, 'This is not the half of it',
We can't wait to grow up a bit,
So people can give us freedom and we can have our bliss,
But until we become adults all we can say,
Is our gang's the best and don't forget it!

Maryam Ali (14)

Knowledge

Knowledge is everything some say,
Knowledge many might fear.
Knowledge is something all should know,
Knowledge is what I hold dear.

People see my glasses, they know I'm smart,
Because of that they call me 'geek'.
They see my eyes move due to a disease,
Because of that they call me 'freak'.

Yet I pay no heed,
To whatever these people say.
I know what I am,
After they repeat things day after day.

What I like adds to my knowledge,
Unnecessary, childish, stupid, I've heard it all.
No matter what people say about me,
I know in the end it is my call.

Knowledge is everything some say,
Knowledge many might fear.
Knowledge is something all should know,
Knowledge is what I hold dear.

Martyn Lees (15)

The Divine Gift

As I walked through the forest on that early spring morn,
The dappled sunlight playfully caressing my face,
I heard an angelic sound that is a divine gift to mortal ears.
The birds, whose song is sweeter than the scent of any flower.
The birds, the music of whom is far more beautiful
                              than that of the heavens above.
The celestial chorus continued, unhesitatingly,
Until they began to sleep.
Then the black sky of night came to mourn the loss
Of such melodious sounds, lost, while the feathered ones slept.
They slept until the next morn when they would once again
                              rival the choirs of Heaven.

Francis Rowney (13)

A Moment In Time

I looked down at the bundle of love,
I had cradled in my arms.
I could feel his tiny hand squeezing my finger.

I could smell the newborn baby smell,
As sweet as roses.
I remember his skin as soft as silk,
His chest rising with every breath he took.

Sitting on the end of my mum's cubicle bed,
Just thinking my life could never get better
Than what it was that very day!

Now he is older I realise life can get better,
And the older he gets the better life is!

Charlotte Marie Adlem (12)

A True Friend

They can heal my pain,
Sometimes if you ask, they lend
A helping hand
As they are my friends

They comfort me when I'm feeling blue,
Crying with me,
Laughing with me
Because they are true.

When I'm alone,
And am in need of someone,
I can ring and ask for them,
They would always run

Across the country,
Over the moon,
They would come to me
Singing a tune.

They may live far,
Like across the sea,
Or maybe near
Like next door to me

Whenever they are blue
I will go to
Their needs, always
Like good friends do.

But when they don't come,
When I'm upset,
It turns out
They're truly not the best!

Harjot Dogra (12)

Jenny

Silently I watch the night,
Hope fading with the light.
The darkness starts surrounding me,
Holding in the pain.

Soon it bursts from me,
Sobs racking the night.
The pain, the anger, the fear.
This is my life,
It's always the same.

My eyesight blurs,
I don't want to go on.
It all seems pointless.
I can't take anymore.

Suddenly she springs,
Drying my tears
With her furry head.
Her green eyes bore into mine,
The pain vanishes.

Softly she begins to purr.
That sounds brings me comfort.
It gets me through.
I know Jenny,
I would not be here,
Without you.

Lorna Mackenzie (16)

Nana

When I think of Nana
I see her happy face,
Smiling because we were there,
Telling us things
About when she was young,
Things she ought not to -
Always full of fun.

A basket in her room,
Always a delight
In the morning full of sweets,
By evening none in sight.
'I didn't eat them all,' she'd say,
'Though I had one or two,
I had plenty of help
From the pair of you!'

When someone you love dies
It feels the world's
About to end.
You can't go on.
People tell you you'll be OK.
Why do they say that?
You know you won't.
Without my nana?
My life's incomplete
Without her,
My great-grandmother.

Louise Mackenzie (11)

Someone Close To Me

She's the toffee in the popcorn,
Sweet and loving.
She's vinegar in the chips,
When angry and bitter.
She's the warmth in the teddy bear,
Comforting and always there.
She's the clearness of the mineral water,
Honest and clean-hearted.
She makes the cold winters to colourful springs,
She makes the autumn leaves to summer shines.
She's like the whirling moon in the evening sky,
She's like the flame-red sun over the cerise meadows.
She's my mum.

Pavetha Seeva (12)

Friends

Most people think that
Everyone needs a best friend
Someone you can trust
And on someone you can depend.

But my group of close friends
Are just as good as one
I can't imagine what I would do
If just one of them had gone.

We have been all different
Right from the start
But I treasure my friends
They're close to my heart.

Rachel Massey (14)

How My Heart Feels

So many things
I don't want to leave
If I had to go
I'd be down on one knee

They'd tug me and tug me
To get in the car
They'd have to get my attention
With an eye-catching star

It would be the fight of a fire
The roaring flames
Separating me from my life
Ablaze with my names

But now I have other thoughts
Set on my mind
How could I see the world
If I were blind?

I'm thankful I have eyes
To see all these things
So many wonders
And what joy it brings

There are so many things
Close to my heart
I just cannot leave them
We won't come apart.

Rebecca Jones (12)

Close To My Heart

They're there for you through thick and thin,
Someone you can lean on,
A shoulder to cry on,
A smile to brighten the darkest days,
Life wouldn't be the same without them,
Friends, a warm fire on a winter night.

A helping hand,
A well kept secret,
Part of one another, their life, your life,
Hearts joined together,
All troubles shared,
Growing stronger together,
Hopes and dreams as one.

Jokes, laughter, tears, shouting,
Falling out never lasts long,
Before a warm hug,
A close chat, thoughts exchanged,
A magic bond, never broken,
A warm heart, a close thought,
Friends.

Claire Grimwade (14)

My Family

First let's start with my mom
She's really great and really fun,
Next up here's my dad
He's wonderful, he makes me glad,
Then there's my brother
And I'm telling you, he's like no other.
I've got aunts, uncles
And cousins as well,
My nans and grandads
Are really swell.
But out of all these put to the test,
I think after all, I am the best!

Gemma Cashmore (12)

The Candle

(In memory of Christopher Knibbs)

Oh candle with your shining light,
Burning in the air so bright,
To me you represent lives that have been lost
And you represent the living.

To me you are a helping hand,
You guide me through the hardest times,
You are there through the tears and laughter
Crying and laughing along with me.

And even when your flame goes out
Your spirit lives on forever.

Hayleigh Louise Knibbs (12)

Flipper

Flipper is blue like the sea
He is sure to be taller than me
He is kind and gentle
Sweet and calm

He is cheeky and sly
As clever as a spy
He eats fish for breakfast
Lunch and tea
He is totally different to me

He swims in the sea
Like a darting missile
Jumps the waves
And splashes about
In the light of the sun,
Drifting.

The sun shone
Like a glistening crystal.

You used to be funny
But now you are boring.

You are my friend
But am I yours?

Jenni Hankinson (12)

My Parents

My parents mean so much to me.
You see, they do everything for me.

But I cannot say they,
For there came a day,
When an accident so tragic,
Used its unfair magic,
To take away no other
Than my dear, caring mother.

Then there's my dad.
He's very quiet,
Always trying to diet.
Giving a helping hand
Of course I won't demand
That he always be there.
I wouldn't dare to disobey,
Well, perhaps I may.

I know I make him mad,
But I'm really not that bad.
Sure I never do any work,
So I always give a smirk,
But at the end of the day I always obey.

I love them both so much.
Mummy had that friendly touch,
Daddy has that helping hand.

So as long as I'm here,
Even when I'm not
They'll always be a part
Of my heart!

Gemma McKenna (13)

How Close?

Guitar
Mum
Guitar, Mum
Guitar, Mum, Mum, guitar
I love 'em both
I love to play new riffs in my room,
It's my music,
My space.
'Can you turn that down?'
That's my mum,
Invading my space.
Can I turn her down, or even off?
Would I want to?
Making me tea,
Cheering me up,
Making me smile,
Telling me off.
My guitar can be absolutely shocking when handled badly.
But then so can my mum.
Guitar, Mum
Guitar, Mum, Mum, guitar?

Mum.

Astrid Brown (14)

Haiku

Love, close to my heart
Money, not close to my heart
Debt means hate not love.

Matthew Maycock (15)

Who Knows?

I would sit in a corner so that I could see everyone and everything.
No one would see me though; I'd be too small to see.
Suddenly, evil would get a taste of its own medicine and I'd be visible.
I'd be completely noticeable, more real than the word itself.

But as soon as evil returns I'd be gone.
Everyone and everything would forget about me.
I'd just be someone sitting in a corner
Watching everyone and everything.
No one would see me though; I'd be too small to see.
Suddenly, evil would get a taste of its own medicine and I'd be visible.
I'd be completely noticeable, more real that the word itself.

Except, this time, they won't forget about me.
I'll make sure of it.
How? Who knows? I would just sit in a corner
So that I could see everyone and everything.
No one would see me though; I'd be too small to see.

Holly Deane (12)

Spot

Spot was a dear old friend
Sadly her old age we could not mend
I remember that I could stroke her when tense
While sitting on my aunt's wooden fence

Back in Spot's day
She would do nothing but play
In that garden supreme
It was Spot's dream

When Spot got older she ran down on energy a tad
And after her walk would sleep in her pad
Spot could eat quite a lot
I remember her eating from a pot

Spot would like nothing better than to be left alone
While chewing on a king size bone
The thing Spot loved was to be a good pet
The thing Spot hated was to go to the vet

Spot was dog to go here and there
And when another dog visited thought that was not fair
All the same Spot would be good
As she knew she would be rewarded with food

Spot was a collie
And loved her toy made of pink folly
Her colour was black and white
And when she barked it would give you a fright

This is near the end of Spot's short story
Of how her death was peaceful not gory
Poor old dog had finally lost the plot
So I write this poem in memory of dear old Spot.

Stuart McKissock (13)

Love Is A Special Thing!

I feel something for you!
I feel like a volcano that's about to erupt.
The lava represents my love for you
Which is contained within my soul.
You make me a better person,
You have made my knees weak
And you have made me whole.

You are now my soul and heart,
If we ever part I will die,
If you break my heart,
It won't be able to heal,
But it will never change the way I feel.

You can't explain love to someone,
They have experience
Love for themselves to understand.
Love is sweet and grand,
But love can get too sweet and turn sour.
Love is something very beautiful like a flower,
When love is broken that flower
Turns into a horrid weed,
But love will always be there because of the seed.

Love is based on affection and trust.
Love isn't based on disloyalty and lust.
There's a saying, treat them mean to keep them keen,
But in my way of thinking
You should get rid of the dust and keep it clean.

Siobhan Savva (13)

The Closest Thing To My Heart

The closest thing to my heart,
I hate it when we're apart.
We love each other till the dying day,
If there's something wrong she will say.

This mysterious person is a wonderful cook,
And has always got her head in some kind of book.
She loves watching *Corrie* and *EastEnders*,
And when she goes shopping she's the last of the big spenders.

She has got lovely blue eyes,
As deep as the skies.
And she's always so cuddly and warm,
I'll make sure that she comes to no harm.

When I am sick she will nurse me back to health,
She does her best even though there's not much wealth.
She goes to college and studies law,
But she only does this so we can have more.

She is doing her test,
And she will do better than all the rest.
She wants to sell the house,
And she makes a cracking pan of scouse.

I know she is a genius and will make me proud,
But when she is angry she shouts really loud.
She hates the rain but likes the snow,
If something is bothering me she will know.

The closest thing to my heart is ... *my mum!*

Carl McGivern (12)

One Man's Land

My home is a place far away,
My home away from the place I stay,
I like to go there when the world
Lays heavy hands upon my heart

My home is defined by only one,
But not a planet, not a sun,
A man, one man does rule this place;
My world revolves around his face

His hands are soft, his eyes are kind,
He comforts when comfort I cannot find,
He's sweet, smiles and never sad
His words come, dissolving all that's bad

If all, like me, had one man's land,
There'd be no need for war,
All would lend a helping hand
And pain would be no more

But not all people, I recall,
When sleep draws close at night,
Can curl their heart up in a ball
To block out pain and fright

One man's land is my escape
From pressures the world must bring
When sky draws tight it's darkened cape,
My life, my love, begin.

Monique Davis (16)

Memories

I miss her eyes, I miss her hair, I miss her friendly smile.
I miss her voice, I miss her hug, I miss her house so kind.
I miss her plates, I miss her food, the way she wore her clothes.
But most of all I miss the way my special time with her
Was wasted, on silly videos, books and toys,
That will always be her.

But I'll remember all the times, it was just her and me
And still I know that, not in body, but in heart and mind,
That's where she'll always be.

These words I write may not make sense, to you, or even to me;
But I know that deep inside they're for her, not you or me.

Sarah Pamenter (12)

A Very Special Lady

A very special lady, with very special ways
Always there to talk to, and help you on sad days

A very gifted lady, with guides from up above
Able to give you evidence, from departed ones - with love

A bright and cheerful lady, a special aura all around
Spreading positive thoughts, to make this world more sound

Now we've lost this special lady, to the spiritual plain,
And each and every one of us is left to feel the pain

We are selfish in our grieving, now that you have gone
What will we do without you? We hope we won't go wrong

A privilege to have known you and be your friend
Our paths will cross again one day, on this we can depend

Goodbye and God bless you, special lady.
Thank you for all you have taught
You made us think so deeply and you will be in our every thought.

James Driscoll (11)

My Mum

The stars in the sky shine brightly,
But they're dim compared to you.
You light up the darkness,
In everything you do.

Even though you're getting older,
You're still so young at heart,
We'll love each other forever,
We'll never, ever part.

You've nursed me since I was a baby,
You've watched me, as I grew,
Isn't it so sad to see,
How quick, time has flew?

We've always had our ups and downs,
And when we feel like lashing out,
But I suppose that's just normal,
That's what life's about.

You probably think I'm sucking up,
But I'm not, this is true.
There's no one in this entire world,
No one quite like *you*.

Kerri Garcha (13)

Close To My Heart

I keep them treasured and valued
In this little heart of mine,
For it contains such wonderful things,
My secrets are safe inside.

My secrets are my true feelings,
Individual and unique,
They are not just in my heart,
But in my soul, down and deep.

These secrets, true and personal
Are as precious as a pearl,
I would cry and be devastated
If they slipped out to the whole wide world.

Locked up safe and sound,
Not told to my friends,
If I had to spill my secrets
My heart just would not mend.

I will hold these secrets forever,
We will never ever part,
The place where they belong
Is close to my heart.

Hanisha Sethi (13)

My Best Friends

Katy, Joanna and of course Vicky,
They are the names of my best friends,
Nothing can ever come between us,
Hoping our friendship will never end.
They're really nice and very kind,
But there is something that lies behind,
Secrets and lies they keep and tell,
But my friendship, I would never sell.
Every time we pass our message book,
Across the classroom to each other,
With the teacher sitting there,
In her head there is no bother.
As days go by and life moves on,
Vicky, Katy and Joanna still belong,
My best friends for evermore,
Especially the memories I do adore.

Emma Cinis (12)

The Closest Thing To My Heart

The closest thing to my heart is my mum.
She's great, she's special, she's my chum.
I know I will always love her forever
And I hope that we always stay together.
She's there when I need her
She's there when I call
She solves all my problems
She gives me her all.
My life is special to her
Her life is special to me
There is a special bond between us,
One you cannot see.

Rachel Tilley (14)

Love

There's a special something inside of us all
Something that loves and cares
This something holds all things
Close to our hearts to share.

Memories are stored here
Of the good and wonderful times
Memories that bring a smile to a face
All of these are good signs.

My friends and family are also stored here
In my special place for them
All are unique and different
Just like finding a rare gem.

Photos are like memories -
Always there to look back upon, to reflect
Seeing happiness upon people's faces
These photos have no defects.

This special something inside of us all
Is stored deep and can never run out
Is symbolised as a heart -
Love, without a doubt.

Laura Evans (14)

The Burning Question

The love I have for you my dear
Is very, very strong
Since I've met you I've lived in fear
Because I'm scared you'll be taken
You're beautiful and funny
I love you very much honey
You're my soul mate
You're punctual and never late
You're so affectionate and loving
You're smart and you make me smile
I've been in love with you for a while
You like the same things as I do
You're dazzling and incredible too
We go on holidays together
To the Bahamas or the Canaries where there's nice weather
You're loyal and nice
And generous and kind
Women like you are hard to find
I would like to have children
But first I have to ask you something
You're a part of my life
So marry me, be my wife.

Elliott Kenton (12)

The Lost Love

If you love me then why did you leave me
I want to see you and hear you
I wanted to kiss you hard but not miss you
You were kind as an angel and sweet as a cherry
I want to be in your sight and see you in the light
I hope to say 'hi' but not 'bye'.

Amir Motlagh (13)

Heartless

What juxtaposes my heart?
Naught, for heart have I none -
Save blood sanguine; veins, flesh and such,
But no heart.
Instead, a tissue festering foul
That once could palpitate, now constricts its innards,
Shrinking.
But halt! What there adjacent resided
Before heart became none?
You did, my love, oh cursed apple,
'Twas you I bit, 'twas me whose substance decreased;
I relished in your thought, now heartless am deceased.

Vanessa Jackson (16)

Close To My Heart

If love is beauty
Then you are too
And if love is blind
Then it's out of sight
And out of mind
Then how can you be with me still
Like hummingbird and daffodil?
Morning doom like damping grass and land
You may be gone but not our love,
Which is here to last!

Saqib Shafiq (12)

Diary

Time goes so slowly
When you've got nothing to do
It seems to take ages
To get the message through

I don't just talk to people
I always speak to my diary
It hasn't got feelings
Not gentle nor fiery

It gladly takes whatever I feel
Awful as it may be
It's not at all fussy
I know it will always see

It never fails to understand
That when I'm down
I need someone to listen
Without a frown

There's nothing worse
Than bottling up fears
Because we all know
It will all end in tears.

Victoria Legge (13)

My Team's Been Relegated!

West Ham has been relegated,
Oh how I hate it.
It seems such a sin,
Excluded from where we have been.
Our players can't wait,
To get out the state,
They have put us in.
For the fans, we'll stay on,
Long after they've gone,
Into the depths of Division One.
After an abysmal season,
I can see no reason,
Why Defoe will get that goal,
No more fancy footwork from Joe Cole,
David James will no longer stay,
While Carrick will go another way.
Oh what a sad, sad day.
But though there'll be strife,
I'll be a Hammer for life.

Kay Davison (15)

Within My Heart

Within my heart,
From which I won't part,
Are my mixed views,
Of love and hate.

Close to my heart,
From which I won't part,
Are my beliefs,
Of what is right and wrong.

Close to my heart,
From which I won't part,
Are my feelings,
Of hope or despair.

Close to my heart,
From which I won't part,
Are my emotions,
From ecstatic to sorrowful.

Close to my heart,
From which I won't part,
Are my thoughts,
Of reflection and ideas.

Close to my heart,
From which I won't part,
Is my passion,
Hope and ambition.

Close to my heart,
It's these I won't part,
Till my heart
Beats no more.

Oliver Butler (14)

What's Close To My Heart?

The amount of things that are close to my heart,
Is completely and absolutely immeasurable.
You've got my dad, intelligent and proud.
You've got my mum, utterly bonkers who loves everyone
And everyone loves her.
Then there's my brothers, two big and one small
And I love them all.
They're my heart's content.
My entire family next and I look up to them all.
A hell of a lot of people, I can tell you!
Like I said ... immeasurable.
And then I've got my sweethearts:
Orlando Bloom and the gorgeous, gorgeous Tom Felton.
He's Draco Malfoy from Harry Potter by the way
And he's fine, fine, fine!
But that's my opinion, I can't refute that.
You'll probably think that's what's close to my heart is weird.
I'll probably think what's close to your heart is weird
You know, sort of like ... vice versa.
But the thing that we really need to consider
Is that what's close to our hearts is priceless
And we don't know what it means to us ...
    ... Until it's gone ...

Laurie Weston (14)

Home Sweet Home

Whenever I look back
I remember the wailing waves
And the deceiving cliffs
Becoming surrendering slaves

To the perilous sea.
I remember my home
Before its fall
Plunging into white foam.

Its nearness to the
Water world
Of water beasts
Before it hurled

Down, down, down.
I remember its familiar smells
The creaky floorboards
And waking church bells.

When I was ill
Or stressed,
Worked up
Or totally messed

There was somewhere
I could indulge my sorrows
And learn
To face my tomorrows.

Even though it has gone forever
It will still remain
Close to my heart
And forever the same.

Because this place
Was my home sweet home.

Maria Rosala (14)

My Grandma

G andma is a wonderful woman,
R ally kind and loving
A d now she's gone to live with God.
N ver shouting or in a huff,
D own the whisky but never drunk!
M ost of all I miss her cuddles
A nd now she's gone to live with God.

Anne-Marie Spiller (15)

Spirit Of The Eagle

I am the spirit of the bird,
And for miles around my cry can be heard,
I have a voice but more I need,
The spirit of the eagle, to make me believe.

It is not my wings that enable me to soar,
But my spirit, the key to the door,
As I rise higher than nature should,
It is not me, but my spirit could.

My spirit is rising, trying to get out,
The only way is to carry on and shout,
But still there is something blocking the way,
No matter how hard I try, no matter how great the day.

If my spirit was to out of me creep,
I could be banished to eternity of sleep,
From the sky I would fall,
And be punished, having to sit on a wall.

I could walk the land, but not rule the sky,
For my spirit would be gone, along with my ability to fly,
I want to keep my spirit from roaming free,
Have tightly locked but not only I hold the key.

Victoria Spencer (11)

The Closest Person Ever To Me

When I feel down and blue,
All I do is talk to you,
No one else can comprehend,
This connection that won't bend.
You have helped me down every road,
And now I think I should thank you loads.
So thank you sister,
You will always be,
The closest person ever to me.

Jess Curitz (14)

My Dolphin Friend

The dolphin glides gracefully through the sea,
He's very intelligent and smiles sweetly at me.
Everyone loves him, he's so strong and so kind,
Just being near him makes you relax body and mind.
He swims through the water, so peaceful and free,
And he jumps into the air and dives back into the sea.
The sun lights the water, which is lovely and clear,
I can almost touch him now, he's getting so near.
His friends come and join him, they play a funny game,
After seeing this creature, my life will never be the same.
They swim for ages, even through the sunset,
I realise what a playful, friendly animal I've met.
He gently nudges my little boat, making it sway,
This is something I won't forget, a really amazing day.
Now it's time to leave, my journey's at an end,
But I will always remember, my lovely dolphin friend!

Becky Denton (13)

My Friend Ellie

I'm all blue inside and feeling real down
I don't want to see anyone, I don't want you around.
I try to tell you to leave me to do this alone
But you say a definite 'no' and won't leave me on my own.

I feel you care
I know you do
I'm feeling lonely and I really need you.
I can't tell you 'I'm dying inside' and 'I need you' to your face
My heart is beating so fast I can't keep the fast pace.

You touch my arm, and give my hair a soft tug
Tears roll down my face and I really need a hug
I want you to hold me and tell me you care
My heart is breaking and I really need you there.

You were there for me
You were there for my pain
I'll always be there for you all the same
To my best friend and very special person
Whenever you're lonely and need a friend
I'll be there for you until the very end.

Bethan Rees-Lewis (15)

Life And You And Me

My stomach goes all funny
When I think of you
When I see you on the telly
My heart, it could just break in two

You're looking so perfect
It's hard for me to see
I will never have your face
Right in front of me.

Life is so uncompromising
Why can't I just see you for a day?
Because everyone else around me
Can't compare to you in any way

You have the best hair
You have the best mouth
Yours are the finest eyes
How I wish all this was lies

Uncompromising…
I'll never find you.

Chloe Day (14)

My Grandma Ivy

My grandma was always so loving and kind,
Another like her, would be very hard to find.
I know she's an angel, in Heaven above,
Sending down blessings and buckets of love.
Her name was Ivy, as I'm sure you all know,
Goodnight, God bless Grandma,
We'll all miss you so.

Love always,
Michaela xxx

Michaela Norwood (13)

Sooty

I wanted you to know
That I love you so,
When we're apart
You remain in my heart,
When I'm feeling low
You just know,
You make me see light again
Completely removing any pain,
Your eyes are my sunrise
And your sparkle never dies,
Sooty you remain true
And I promise I will too!

Laura Dalton (13)

Love

Love is a story that's never been told,
Love is a song that's never been sung,
Love is a question that's never been answered,
Love is a rose that never sleeps,
Love is a part of you, that cannot be explained,
Love is like a river where your feelings flow out,
Love is a poem that hasn't been written, until now,
Because love is like lightning,
You never know when it's going to strike.

Stephanie Brown (13)

My Mum . . .

My mum is as soft as a sofa waiting to be sat on,
As sweet as a lemon bonbon,
Always there for me,
She's like the lock and I'm the key,
My mum always makes me smile,
For a long while,

My mum is as luxurious as a living room,
And still has time to sweep and broom,
When I am really sad,
She cheers me up and makes me glad,

My mum is as soft as a rabbit,
With no bad habit,
As happy as Larry,
And deserves a queen's carry!

My mum is as sunny in the morning,
As the break is dawning,
And as happy at night,
(This often gives me a fright!)

My mum is as frothy as a cappuccino,
And as readable as the comic Beano,
She is my friend,
Even when I drive her round the bend!

My mum has a heart of gold,
That never could be sold,
My mum's as nice as pie,
It brings a tear to my eye.

Victoria Lomax (12)

Who Cares?

Who's the one who cares for me?
Is it my parents, God, a friend or just me?
Who's the one who loves me so?
Oh please tell me,
I wish that I know.

All the hate in the world today,
Is so bad, I think that it might decay.
What happened to the world so nice and sweet?
But now it is all hate and defeat.
Wars break out and people get killed,
Just for the sake of being greedy.

Let me ponder on what I have just said,
Is it all true or lies instead?
To me I feel it's mostly true,
But the same one must love both me and you.

Kerry McCathie (14)

You Ask Me What Is Dear To Me

You ask me what is dear to me,
A person, a pet, a memory,
But I can't choose, I have so many,
Family, friends, my lucky penny,
So I am now going to write
About everything in my sight,
All the things I hold in my heart,
All the things from which I can never part,
Firstly there's my family,
Who always put their trust in me,
My friends who always are around,
When I needed help it was them I found,
My hamster Rocky is so sweet,
When he stands up and begs me for a treat.
My photos that remind me of special things,
More precious to me than diamond rings.
The necklace I got from a special mate,
The flowers I got on my first ever date,
The book I got for my confirmation,
My phone - the best line of communication!
You asked me what is dear to me,
And hopefully now you will see,
There are many things in this old heart,
Things from which I can never part.

Rhian Owen (14)

My Island

Majorca is my favourite place,
Fourteen times I've been.
It's like my second home as I know it well:
All the towns and places I've been.

Each Easter me and my family go
To Pollenca Park Hotel.
It's really friendly with loads to do,
And just 2 minutes from the beach as well.

The scenery everywhere is breathtaking;
It's picturesque and beautiful.
From golden sands to sparkling seas,
There's nowhere that's unattractive or dull.

I love walking in the mountains
On a clear, cloudless day.
I am taken away from reality
To a paradise where I wish I could stay.

Pam Bustard (14)

Affinity

I've lived my life in wretched silence; you helped me speak.
I've walked with my eyes tight shut; you opened them for me
I've listened without hearing, but your voice rings in my ears
I want to scream my love for you for all the world to hear
I want to let them know that I feel safe with you so near.
You've lit a candle inside of me and it burns now deep within
If I opened up my mouth to speak the light would pierce my skin
Illuminating my secrets of how I feel for you,
I was surprised at how quickly my love for you grew
Now I try to escape as I walk too close to the edge again.
Days make no sense, think I'm going crazy, might be going insane
I'm slowly spinning around, yet quickly falling down
In my heavy and confusing emotions, I begin to drown
In a world that will never truly understand
I could never walk the streets holding your hand
But this life would mean nothing without you here beside me
I'm giving in to this power that has enraptured me
My life revolves around you; you are my hidden addiction,
I want to know your innermost wishes and your darkest convictions
You could be the one that I will always love
You should be the one that I will always love
You will be the one that I will always love.

Aimee Smith (15)

My Red And White Wizards

Wicked, cool and fab,
Kicking the ball with precision,
Aiming to score the vital goal,
To beat the opposition.

Neil Warnock - he is the man,
Always inspirational,
Manager extraordinaire
He really is a sensation.

And Paddy Kenny - what a goalie,
Arms outstretched and focused,
Peshisolidio aiming a header,
To put the Blades in the lead - yes!

Allison just misses the goal post,
Jags skids off pitch,
Sarbs flicks the ball to Windass,
Monty spectacularly sprints to receive.

Tonge leaps in mid-air as if jet-propelled,
Nuddy covers the pitch with such ease,
And Kozzy, joker of the team
With his easy to see ginger hair,
Browny, the ace king of scoring the goals.

Kabba always has a trick up his sleeve,
Curtis, likes to have possession of the ball,
And Macca has his strategists head on,
While Pagey makes sure the opponents cannot score,
Sheffield United - my heroes, they reign supreme!

Louise Thackeray (12)

I'll See You Again Some Day . . .

Phone call late at night, for my mum who was in the shower,
this made us all worry, cos she was on there for at least half an hour.

Grandad had been feeling dizzy, then he'd had an attack,
lucky he was now in hospital, but we didn't know if he'd be back.

We didn't know what was happening, that made me feel sad,
a horrifying experience, losing my grandad.

Though I didn't want to, I had to go to school,
sent a letter to my teacher, talking him through it all.

Still alive in hospital, going through each hour,
getting worse each moment, losing all his power.

Then really early in the morning, received another phone call,
'Get down to the hospital.' I didn't know what was happening at all.

My brother and me round my other nan's, to spend all day,
Mum and Dad at the hospital, all we could do was pray.

We knew this was the time, Grandad was to go,
the angels would take him to Heaven, we still kept saying no.

Crying through my pain, though memories will never fade,
he really was it all, a good friend I had made.

The next event to happen, the chance to say goodbye,
the funeral, I'd probably just cry.

He's now gone forever, life'll never be the same,
great man to have lost, I'll always remember his name.

All this thinking of past memories, one day we'll meet again
I can't wait to see him, dissolve all of this pain . . .

Kristina Fleuty (13)

It

The thing that is most close to me,
I hold dearly in my heart,
I've had it since I was a child,
And with it I shall never part.

It comforts me when I am sad,
Finds me when I am lost,
Assures me when I'm in fear
And calms me when I am cross.

But it's not just there for me,
When I'm sad or in sorrow,
It's there for me day and night,
Yesterday, today, tomorrow.

It's there for me when I am happy,
Or when I have been bad,
It joins me in my laughter
And makes me feel so glad.

It's trusted me with secrets,
Which I'll hold to the bitter end,
But 'it' is not an 'it' at all,
Because 'it' is my dearest friend.

Jamie Wilyman (12)

Gareth Gates, I Love You!

Gareth Gates, I love you,
Yes, oh yes, I really do.
With your continuous courage,
Right from the start,
Your gorgeous speech,
It touched my heart.
Your angel face
And your remarkable voice,
I idolise you,
You're my first choice.

You're on my bedroom wall,
For evermore,
Because it's you,
That I adore.
I listen to you,
All of the time,
You are always on my mind.

My favourite of your songs,
Is *Stupid Mistake,*
Because I know,
It's really great
And when you're in my heart,
It will never break.

When I'm down I listen to you
And I can do anything,
That I try to do.
Gareth Gates, I love you,
Yes, oh yes, I really do!

Jessica Birch (12)

No Worries

My friends are near, they will always be here,
Especially to my heart, I hold them dear,
Through thick and thin they will remain,
Through hot temperatures and the coldest rain,
We have our arguments to put our opinions in frame,
To keep us apart is to remain insane,
We are a band of fellow beings that show affection,
In our own way we show friendship in a mirror reflection.

We never know what may be happening,
We cannot tell what will come, we will know it's something,
Something good, sad, glad, mad?
We'll face it together, good or bad,
We love spending time together,
Will we remain friends forever?
We're all different in our own way,
We bring in our specialities and leave our problems at bay,
But hey, we're friends, we like each other's company,
If our personalities were built up like a tower,
It wouldn't wobble for it was cemented together with friendship power.

Frank Osborne (14)

Granda

Now you're gone I had to say
I miss you greatly, every night and day
To show I care, I cry and pray
Because you cuddled me when I was mad,
You dried my tears when I was sad.
No matter what, I still love you
'Cause you're my bestest friend
And even though we're miles apart
You will always remain close to my heart,
Granda.

Rachel Doherty (14)

The Lament Of A Mother

It's hard work to be a mother
Cleanin' up, what a bother
The thing is we don't get paid,
Sometimes I wish I had a maid.

I can wash, I can cook
Without looking at the book,
Dirty dishes, dirty clothes,
Cookin' meals on the kitchen stove,
I go shopping I come home
An' I'm left all alone.

Walk the dog round and round,
But I can't let him go to the pound,
Washin' and scrubbin',
Cleanin' and rubbin',
Where am I going to?
When I have more work to do,
They're all at school, I'm at home,
The dog's OK, he sits and chews a bone.

One's eleven the other's thirteen,
Why can't they keep their rooms clean?
I would love some time,
That I can call mine,
Butterin' bread, butterin' scones,
Within a few minutes they're all gone.

I want peace, I want quiet,
Without worrying about their diet,
To think of me and me alone,
To ensure some peace I'll unplug the phone,
The thing is we don't get paid,
Sometimes I wish I had a maid!

Erin Rebecca Black (14)

The Manchester United Team

It's Ryan Giggs on the ball
Will he pass or will he score?
He passes it to Paul Scholes,
Paul Scholes flicks the ball over an Everton defender,
To van Nistelrooy.
He shoots it in the goal 2-1 up, but when 90 minutes is up
You will cheer, as Man Utd is given the Barclaycard
Premiership Cup as we cheer them on!

Luke Brown (14)

Close To My Heart

I had a little hamster,
It liked to look around,
It liked to run a lot
And never tired down.

It always crawled on your head,
You could have a laugh with it.

Until one day it died.

I loved my little hamster,
I will never forget it.

Emma Bunday (13)

A Springy Thingy

My dog's a springy thing,
She bounces up and down
And when it's time to feed her,
She'll run round and round.

If you try to leave her,
She dashes up the stair
And when you try and call her,
She won't come down from there.

As soon as you go near her lead,
She goes absolutely crazy
And when you calm her right back down,
She goes really lazy.

To describe my dog in a couple of words,
Would be tough but not impossible.
I think it would be
A springy thingy.

Lloyd Evans (12)

My Cat

My cat is cuddly and furry
She looks like caramel and cream.

She looks around the ground
Purring all day long.

Then she sleeps for an hour or two
Then she goes to get some food.

Then she starts running around the house
And that's because I love her.

Jessica Church (11)

Shelley

She was found in a bag,
She was only a few days old.
She was six months older than me when I was born.
We grew up together,
She was more like a sister to me.
She liked to have her neck scratched,
Or her head tickled.
She was one of my best friends.
When we grew older,
We grew apart.
School work was more important,
I didn't have time to play.
But one day she was gone.

On the 2nd February 2003 she died.
I wasn't there when she died,
I was at my friend's house,
Having a good time.
I didn't tell her I loved her.
Did she know?
I hope so.
I loved my cat called Shelley,
I will always remember her.
She was one of my best friends
And will be my best friend . . .
Forever.

Sarah Harris (15)

Strong Love

Together forever me and my love
Like two married angels up high above
I feel strong feelings for this person I adore
Like a fluffy rabbit you have to care for
Or maybe man and dog when their friendship never ends.
I don't know whether it's me
But I think we are more than friends
When we are apart I feel like I am in pain
I feel like this for hours until he's back again.
I have this deepness of passion locked up into my heart
It's swirling around inside my body like a work of art
We love each other ever so much
As I have written you have already sussed
I love him, he loves me
Together forever that's us.

Natasha Herbert (12)

Pathetic Fallacy

The sun had helped me stay awake
Although my mind was tired and sleepy, I felt weak
And everything around me seemed fake.
I've often thought of you these past few weeks,
Including once or twice today
While sun was shining, like last May
When we had been so close. Then evening came,
The wind picked up. I thought of you somehow,
And sent a text that was quite lame,
That hid my feelings well. I don't regret it now,
Perhaps I should, perhaps I will …
I gave up waiting, for - though I wait still -
I realised you weren't going to call.
Right then, the rain started to fall.

Nikita Alatortsev (16)

Close To My Heart

Close to my heart is my cat,
He is so much better than the rest:
He is friendly and cool,
But sometimes cruel
Falco Sidwell,
But he will always be close to my heart!

Close to my heart are my friends,
Especially because our friendship never ends:
They make me laugh at Wootton Bassett School
Because they are friendly and cool,
That is why they are close to my heart!

Close to my heart are my family,
Mum, Dad, two brothers, two nanas
And one grandad and all the rest:
They're always there when I am down,
They always take away my frown.
They're the cool people from the block,
They're never out of loving stock,
My heart is empty without them.
They are, oh they are,
The Sidwell family.
Closer than ever, closer than before,
Close to my heart.

Natasha Sidwell (12)

The Hidden Message

The angel came to me in the middle of the night
And sang a song with words so bright,
I asked her, 'Why do you sing?'
'Because peace to my heart, it does bring.'
'What can bring peace close to my heart?'
'Excitement and happiness, you should never part,'
'But what does all this mean?'
'Don't be so over keen, just live your life and you will know,
Who could be your friend and who will be your foe.'

Helena Singleton (12)

If You

If you were a summer's day
You would chase the clouds away.

If you were an evening star
You would be the brightest one by far.

If you were a great big book
I'd know exactly where to look.

If you were in the sky above
You would be the only one I'd love.

If you were as sweet as can be
You would be the only one I'd want to see.

If you and me were to meet
I would sweep you off your feet.

If you were a little tree
Even then you would be the one for me.

If you were to always care
I would always be there.

Danielle Barlow-Exton (12)

Snowy

Snowy,
Her fur as white as fresh, crisp snow,
Her eyes twinkle like diamonds in the moonlight,
She purrs affectionately as I stroke her in the early morning sun,
Then settles down for a nap.

I awake in the morning to find she's not there,
I search the house and the garden,
I find her under the shed,
Her fur is no longer as white as fresh, crisp snow,
Now it is as red as a rose, blood-red.

I cradle her in my arms as Mum gets dressed,
We rush her to the vet's,
Her eyes no longer twinkle,
There's nothing they can do,
But put her to sleep.

My Snowy has gone ... forever
But my love for her will never cease.

Charlotte Elizabeth Burch (12)

Far But Near

I love you so I miss you,
I'd kiss you but you're far,
Driving away from here,
In your long, blue Rover car.

Your melody will get to me,
From far-off, scary lands,
Where you have travelled,
Over evil seas and sands.

Forever I'll be sorry,
For love to act like this,
I know you can't forgive me,
But please remember our bliss.

We're still together, though far away,
Sitting on a rooftop,
I remember you'd once say,
I love you more every day.

Katie Rose Palfreeman (13)

My Weekly Routine

My alarm goes off, oh no it's Monday morning
'What you doing?' my mother always says. 'No time for yawning.'
Time for boring old school
You must be mad if you think it's cool
Work, work, work is all we do
Then horror strikes when you haven't got a clue
You have no life when teachers set you homework
And your brother has none and gives you a smirk
Finally home time you can watch some telly
When you see Ready Steady Cook then you get a rumble in your belly
At least you can have a choice unlike school dinners
Dinner ladies say, 'Don't forget you're sinners.'
What? I couldn't think of anything to rhyme
Good God 10:30, is that the time?
Time to go to bed
My pillow is like a magnet, it sticks to my head
Comes to a Wednesday the middle of the week
When all your clothes start to reek
That's when Mum and Dad are always there
To wash and dry your underwear
Thank God it's Friday the beginning of the weekend
I can show-off the latest trend
I can hang with my mates
I can't think why they like to offer me cakes
How nice it's Sunday
I live on a farm and it's my time to collect all the hay
Another week over another one begun
At the minute my older brother is chasing me so I have to run
If your schedule is as hectic as mine,
I would like to see you try and make it rhyme.

Wenonah Whalley (14)

Close To My Heart

Close to my heart,
Is where he stays,
If anyone talks about him,
That person pays.

His lovely smile,
It is so dear,
If I can't boast about him,
I shed a tear.

He's captured my heart
And it's like a door,
He walks in and out,
Tramps on the floor.

It seems so silly,
But he drives me crazy,
If I see him,
My limbs go lazy.

I can't sleep at night,
I daydream all day,
I'm in another world,
Far, far away.

It's not just a crush,
It's really true love,
I'm his turtle
And he's my dove.

Together forever,
That's what it'll be,
In my heart always,
His spell cast on me.

Nadine McFarland (14)

It

I lie in my bed, knowing it will come.
It silently slips through my door,
Like an eerie gust of wind blowing through the leaves of a tree.
It glides across the floor like a shadow, then, I hear the creak
Of the floorboards.
This sound is familiar to my ears.
I close my eyes and lie still.
I hear the *bump*, as it pounces on my sheets.
It flies up to my face like a plastic bag
Caught in an updraught of wind.
I grit my teeth, a wet slice hits my face and penetrates my stillness.
I writhe around as a flurry of cold, wet slaps hit my face.
I shake it off and slowly stroke its fur,
As I repeat the same words every night,
'You can't go to the park now you daft dog!'

Tom Harris (13)

My Little Brother

My little brother runs about all day and night
And wakes me up with a fright.
He plays with his toys
And makes a lot of noise.

At night his tiny devil comes out in the form of a small cloud
And makes my brother cry out loud,
My mum or dad wake up all tired and cranky,
To fetch a bottle of milk to make him happy.

Even though my brother acts like a chimpanzee
And he drives me crazy,
I love him enough,
To make him love me.

Absher Mansoor (12)

My Family

I love my mum, I love my dad,
They are the best parents anyone's had.

My mum's quite tall and pretty thin,
But when she smiles it's a great big grin.

My dad's very funny and never sad,
When he cracks a pun they're really bad.

I have a guinea pig called Rosie,
In her hutch she's very cosy.

I have two cats called Irish and Benny,
I wouldn't exchange them for even a penny.

I love my mum, I love my dad,
They are the best parents anyone's had.

Rory O'Brien (13)

Kitty

There he sits outside
Through the rain, the snow, the sun, the cold
Do you see him?
Alone he sits staring in through the window
Looking in at me as he miaows.
I go out to feed him
He jumps down from the boiler house
He seems to greet me
He rubs my legs with his soft fur
And looks innocently at me with his wide eyes
I pet him as I feed him
He is happy to see me
And I am grateful to have Kitty.

Stephanie Carroll (12)

Me And My Grandad

He is my dream grandad
When I'm with him I'm never sad.
We make a perfect team
Just like strawberries and cream.
We have lots of fun together
No matter what the weather.
Grandad tells some very good jokes
His only fault is that he smokes.
He's getting old, he's seventy-one
But still working hard, alongside his son.
He works at the garage every day
And never ever likes going away.
He's been married to Nan for nearly fifty years
They've had lots of laughs - and a few tears.
Two children, four grandchildren, lots of friends
The love of my grandad never ends.
He's very special to me
And I know he always will be.
He's the best grandad in the world
And I love him very much!

Harriet Reynolds (12)

My Family

My family are important to me
It's like we have a guiding key
Seeing them happy and making them laugh
Some might be brainy and some might be daft
Nevertheless they're my family
And my family are important to me!

Courtney Hemstritch (12)

A Wintry Wood

A cold chill swoops
Through the glimmering branches
Icicles freeze the blood off trees
Birds plod against the frozen snow
Looking for worms, berries and other foods
Foxes plod against the entwining coldness
Snow kills little creatures
Blackbirds and robins nest in the hollows
And eat the berries on the dazzling branches
Rivers and ponds freeze over
Still having a gust of wind over them
Killing the animals in the rivers and ponds
Frozen trees
The treecreeper hurries up the tree
And hides in the hollow branches
The trees stand proud even in winter.

Jessica Richardson (15)

At The Seaside

Water of blue
Waves of green
In the sea it is green
But on the ship they're so keen
Elegant green fingers
Swirling, whirling
Dancing on the seashore
Swimming in the sea.
Here comes a shark
Help me, save me
Here comes a lifeguard
And he saved me!
Gigantic seagulls
Swooping to the sea
Just to catch some nice tea.
The best time ever
Hope to go again.

Ashleigh Stevens

What Am I?

Sitting on the sofa all of the time,
Arguing with my sister shouting, 'It's mine.'

Watching TV or playing on the PC,
Writing letters that parents don't want to see.

Doing homework while on the phone,
Going to school always on my own.

Fussing and worrying all about spots,
While eating lots and lots of chocs.

What am I, a big red pie?
No, a teenager that is I.

Pippa Batey (12)

The World And I

I can't run or leap
Stay small or tall
I can't peep or weep
Wake or sleep
I wouldn't change it
For the moon, the stars
Or posh new cars
I love the world
And the world loves me.
But the world and I don't always see eye to eye.
I promise you I can take it
I see all of us
All I see
Do you know who I am?
I am the sky
The world and I
On whom you do rely.

Bryony Milliken (11)

Spells

Head of dog, eye of frog,
Mixture from a bubbling bog.
Eye of cat, toe of rat,
Wings from a flying bat,
Pig's squeal, car wheel
The electric from an electric eel
Sting of bee, bite of flea,
Skin of a leopard that's wild and free.

Hubble, bubble, double trouble,
Ugly sisters, difficult blisters.

Wasp sting, bird's wing,
We'll put in almost everything,
Fire ash, scabs off a rash
Put in potato, especially mash,
Grime off bin, shove it in,
Add in one fish fin
This potion is made for me and you
That's if I don't eat you too.

Hubble, bubble, double trouble,
Ugly sisters, difficult blisters.

Vicky Scott (13)

Medieval War
A Knight

Through the battlefield I ride
On my noble steed
Honour will be my guide
Doing my country's deed.

Swords shining in the sun
Even in the night
Bravery will be my gun
For my kingdom I will fight.

On horseback I stride
Across the distant land
Where many men have died
As if peace was banned.

As if shields weren't enough
I'm the worlds greatest knight
You've got to be tough
For my king I will fight.

Daniel Pierce (12)

As I Walk

As I walk through the death traps,
Walking in the cold, muddy trenches,
Walking through the screams of death and destruction,
Walking through the stench of corpses and rotting flesh,
Walking past the bombs and shooting,
Walking past the shouting and crying of young men,
I see no glory in their faces,
No pride, no greatness because they are fighting for their country,
I see only pain,
Pain and suffering of young men.
Can you tell me this is right?

Stephanie Bartle (13)

If I Could Change . . .

If I could change the world today
I'd use my mind to work and play
My power, my will, my mind now
Those things I would change but how
I'd solve foolish quarrels and fights
And replace them with childish delights
War would be a thing of the past
And there would be peace in the world at last
I would get rid of sadness completely
And everyone would be treated the same and freely
People who don't have money would still amount
Because it's what's inside that really does count
Disabled people stand up and say
I am free . . . I live . . . hooray!
Animals would run off hunting ranges
This is my world with my changes.

Danny Hounslow (12)

One Day

One day I would like to travel far,
something I'd really love.
To go on an expensive hol -
but not by car!
A place where palm trees grow high
and tropical birds can be seen.
Where hours are spent under the sun,
that's my holiday dream.
The hotel would be marble white,
the sea would be sparkling clean,
the sound of cicadas would fill the night.
The waves on the sea would be gentle,
the sand would be powdery soft.
The moon would shine on the sea at night
like a silver medallion.

Jessica Bull (13)

My Tortoise

Brown, green coloured all over
A tail, little, pointed, small
My tortoise's tongue is dry and cold
A mouth that shows just a little expression
My tortoise in the morning is a small, dozy shadow
After I have slept there's my tortoise
Not moved very far but still there in the morning
Greets me slowly, tilts its head
First out of the shell a wrinkly head, four feet and a teeny tail
Still dozy, wanders around the garden
Looking for something tasty for breakfast
My tortoise goes, it's time for bed
It sleeps for months like it's locked in jail
The shell locks my tortoise inside
It is a hibernator, for months it must sleep
My tortoise cheers me up inside
Makes me burn, makes me feel glad
My most special thing
Looks just normal
But underneath its shell is a golden star.

Frances Leanne Busson (11)

Close To My Heart

I have a friend called Squeaky,
Who lives in my bedroom at night.
Sometimes Squeaky can be a bit smelly,
Until I clean out her bed.

Squeaky is my friend and I love her a lot,
I play with her and make her little toys.

Once when I was playing,
Squeaky didn't seem to move.
I looked at Squeaky more closely
It can't be true, I'm sure it's not,
It is - my Squeaky's dead!

My mum and dad got me a new Squeaky,
But she simply is not the same.

I cried and cried all night,
I couldn't stop thinking about Squeaky.
Why did she have to leave me?
I'm so lonely without her!

Rebecca Bootman (11)

Dillon And Hazel

Dillon was her Romeo
She was Juliet,
He was big and she was small,
Their married life was set,
They had so many escapades,
Their life was full of fun,
They often spent many days
Basking in the sun.
Their greatest love was flowers,
(They ate them all day long)
The garden was their special place,
Where the birds chirped out a song
But like in Shakespeare's famous yarn,
The star-crossed lovers die,
They still eat the plants,
(From underneath)
Where my sweet rabbits lie.

Beth Georgiou (12)

Friends

F   is for friends who stick together
R   is for reliability
I   is for ice cream which friends share
E   is for enjoyment when you're together
N   is for never let each other down
D   is for dearest friend
S   is for sharing things with each other.

Lauren Scanlon (12)

Dearest Brother

At first I didn't understand, but now I do
Lots of pictures and images of us, but hardly any of you
There are times when I don't feel loved and it makes me truly sad
He has never shown you love, it must really hurt you bad
There's not much that I can say because it won't change the past
But if we rebuild our bond, I hope and pray that it will last
I know why you were mean to me, my heart is filled with guilt
He washed away your soul and made you feel like silt
Three children born and you are his first
Every time you tried to make things better it only made it worse
I was naive and believed, Daddy could do no wrong
But then I began to realise how he treated his only son
Right about now, I'm having problems of my own
And for the first time, we can relate - we're both alone
When I look in the mirror at my reflection and then look into your eyes
I see the pain that we both feel - the pain you still deny
We're both a little older and I'm no longer blinded by perception
I'm too tired to be a part of his games and too wise for his deception
Many years we lost between us, because of your pain
Caused by this man
Dear brother please believe me, I didn't understand
So if it's not too late, let's make jokes and drown our tears in laughter
We're old enough to realise he does not want to be a father
So now I understand you, you're no longer in the dark,
I thought I'd let you know that you are close to my heart.

Natasha Williams (14)

Soul Food

The most special thing in the world to me
You'd never be able to find,
It's my soul right deep down, sealed forever
Locked in my heart, closed in my mind

My soul is different because it can
Help see things from different views,
It's taught me a lot, how to care and love
And put myself in others' shoes

For a soul to do this it must be fed
With great advice from your mates
And your family put love and protection in,
Not a drop of it goes to waste

As life goes by, you never stop learning
Which is why I've realised that,
To succeed you just follow your soul
And step onto the believing mat

Sometimes others will cruelly put you down,
They're the jealous ones with closed eyes,
They don't always realise what they've done
Your soul helps you stay strong and wise

People try to mess with your emotions
But find you're never giving in,
'Cause no matter what they say or do
It's a game they'll never win

My family and friends strengthen my soul
By loving: a wonderful art
They help me through whatever life will throw
Which is why they are close to my heart

Never feel alone on this Earth,
Let people know just how much you're worth!

Sascha Williams (13)

Close To My Heart

Close to my heart
the things dearest to me
are sacred and true
are honoured and free
full of sentiment
I glorify each
a certain nobility
arises, in each
and so these things dearest
dearest to me
close to my heart
they'll stay for eternity.

Charlotte Dare (12)

Close To Me

A peace of mind is closest to me,
It's a special thing that makes me be,
It's a fickle world seen through my eyes,
It's a cool wind that tells no lies.

It's an ongoing horizon that's always there,
It's a time to stop, stand and stare.

It's the art of escapism from everyday life,
It's a way of coping with any strife.

It's expression of self that makes you whole,
It's that harmonious moment when you're attuned to your soul.

Ross Daniels (14)

My Chest Of Dreams

Inside my little treasure chest,
there lies a million dreams.
So many little things, but what
a lot they mean to me.

Inside my little treasure chest,
there lies a bracelet from my friend.
It represents our friendship,
one that will never end.

Inside my little treasure chest,
there lies a kiss from my sweetheart.
A whole year we've been together,
let's hope we will never part.

Inside my little treasure chest,
there lies a photo of my family.
We've been through so much,
I thank them for my life eternally.

Inside my little treasure chest,
there lies a wish for my years ahead.
I can't wait to face the world and
live for the day, like Mum said.

Inside my little treasure chest,
there lies a million dreams.

Inside my little treasure chest,
there lies my life and me.

Jayde Sayers (12)

It's Not The End

(In memory of Frances McCann)

For you it's not the end just the start,
Hitting another target exactly like a dart.
Now you're gone and everyone is sad,
Yet going to Heaven makes you glad.

There will always be you in our hearts,
For we all can't bear to be apart.
Still there might be some strange joy,
As they say, it doesn't have to be the real McCoy.

Sooner or later we'll all be with you there,
Sitting in the clouds without a care.
God shall still love us all,
In this world shaped like a ball.

Yet still this pain will fade away,
Because in our hearts you'll always stay.
Years roll by as we grow old,
We'll be with you when our bodies are cold.

For you it's not the end just the start,
Hitting another target exactly like a dart.

Denise M Bennett (12)

Special Memory

You were once here alongside me,
It was as good as it could be,
Your warm smile glowing,
Kept the cool rivers flowing,
Till the stars did twinkle
And the church bells jingled.

You were once here alongside me,
You were my happiness' key.
Your gentle touch,
Still in my clutch,
We watched the birds fly high,
But still the time is ticking by.

You were once here alongside me,
But now you fade in my loving memory.

Kerrie Bath (13)

The Special Person

A safety blanket
A warmth in winter
A light in the dark
A giver of life
An unconditional love
The one I love
My mum.

Emma Jane Tilney (13)

Faded Memories

The memories that I once treasured,
Are slipping from my hands;
Slipping through my fingers,
Like tiny grains of sand.

Memories of loved ones,
Who have now passed away.
The images I see of them
Get fainter by the day.

I hate that I forget these things,
That once had meant so much.
Memories of old school friends,
Who'd sworn to stay in touch.

But the memories that I once treasured,
Have slipped out of my hands;
Slipped between my fingers
Like tiny grains of sand.

Emma E MacDonald (14)

For Nick

Whichever the direction of the tide;
Whatever the wind may bring;
Whatever keeps the embers burning;
Whatever the birds may sing,

I will always love you,
Come water, wind, earth or fire
And I will bring you all the love
And everything your heart desires.

Alice Thickett (14)

How Can That Be . . . My Dad?

How can that be my dad? How can he walk like that?
Walking all around town, prancing like a cat.
Feet are all turned inwards, legs are bendy too,
He always thinks he's really tall, though he's only five foot two!

How can that be my dad? Why does he stand like that?
Always hands in pockets and wears a silly hat.

How can that be my dad? Why does he drive like that?
I don't know who he thinks he is, maybe Postman Pat.

How can that be my dad? Why does he shout like that?
He used to read me stories and feed our neighbours' cat.
Now he just plays football, watching TV too,
I have to keep on telling him that he's not twenty-two.

In the field he lays, then he climbs a tree,
Everyone laughing, not at him but at

me!

Then I realise what he's done,
Laughing and playing, just having fun.
I've got to remember he's my dad
And isn't really all that bad!

Laura Price (13)

Marilyn Monroe

Some Like It Hot, or so they say,
I wonder if she liked it that way,
The Seven Year Itch it's what she got,
Especially with those skirt blowing shots,
Yet she was still depressed, alone,
She was a Jean Harlow wannabe clone,
Sex symbol, platinum-blonde hair,
Men can't help but stop and stare,
Her past was bleak, she was a fighter,
Her future got brighter and brighter.
There's no business like show business, that's quite true,
Marilyn Monroe got bit in the back, given the flu.
Gentlemen Prefer Blondes, or so I'm told,
So why did she keep being left in the cold?
As I look on, from afar,
I see her, the great star,
She's my idol, now that's a fact
And she knew how to act.
She had a bleak childhood, often wanted to cry,
Soon she was learning how to wave goodbye.
Marilyn Monroe struggled on
And looked what she stumbled upon.
So look at her there,
I want to be like her, if I dare.
She is so very special that I say
And when she died, oh what a dark day.
Many out there want to be her and I'm just another one,
But nothing can compare to who she was,
No one can be her,
Marilyn Monroe.

Jayne Pearson (15)

Close To My Heart

(For Grandad)

I can picture you there

The hall is bursting
With bubbles of laughter and cheer
There's a frenzy of joy spiralling high
Everyone feels so passionately peaceful and free
Meeting old friends and encountering new.

A table groans with unimaginable delicacies
For all the nations that are mingled there
The angelic music is just perfectly pure
You can twirl to a tango, jump to a jive
With endless energy you never had before.

It's your dream paradise

Now that you're gone I've realised
What a wonderful person you were
Nothing will replace the times we shared
No one will know you like I did

So when I'm feeling down, I know you're up there
Laughing that hearty chuckle
And I feel you watching
And somehow I sense your warm gentle arms around me
Then I keep going and trying hard
Knowing how pleased you would be

I'm just glad you are happy
And I want to let you know
You're so special
You'll be close to my heart forever.

Anne Moore (14)

Friends

Think of all the things friends do for you,
Sometimes the things they don't.
They try to smile, to make you laugh
Even if you won't.

Think of all the things they've said or done,
The times when they've been there,
To give support or comfort
And to show you that they care.

Think of when you're sad or lonely
And you feel there's no way out
They'll always want to help you
For that's what friends are all about.

Who are the ones who remain so strong,
Even when you're not,
Thinking about it my friends are
One of the best things I've got.

Sometimes you may lose patience
And feel the need to disagree
But if you're able to work through it
Then you're the best friend you can be.

Sometimes you'll both want different things
And won't admit you're in the wrong
But if you try to swallow your pride
You'll once more get along.

I know my friends won't always be there
To catch me when I fall
But I'd rather live one day with friends
Than a life without any at all.

Marietta Longley (13)

Close To My Heart

I support Manchester United because they are the best
Sure, they lose sometimes, but no one can test their skill, their shots
The players they have, no one can beat United, they're just too bad!

There are millions of players around the world like Raul Zidane
And Figo
But none come close to sheer skill of Rudd van Nistelrooy
and Beckham

Others may think differently but others may think the same
I know he's not the best in the world but his scoring record's insane!

'He shoots, he scores, he shoots, he scores,' it's all the
                                        commentators say
Then they say, 'There he goes again, he always puts the ball away!'

You know I am really thankful to have players like that in my team
You know the ones who always score, so we win the cup and the league

We weren't always this good and it's only this season we've won
But players in the past like Cantona have made sure we always
Come first

But the credit must go to Fergie you know, the one that Wenger hates
Our manager has got us so far and will never turn away
From the people at Old Trafford who will always be there

Now it is time to go but I just want to let you know there is no
Better team than United
So come join the family of United fans all over the world.

Mandeep Khamba (12)

Mothers

(Dedicated to Mrs G Adams - My mum)

Some people may laugh at this
And think it is really soppy.
But that means their mum isn't as great as mine,
For that reason, I am sorry.

Sorry that your mum does not understand you
And does not give you space.
Sorry that she did not care for you
And wipe food from your face.

Mums, mummies and mothers are all fantastic,
They know how to make you smile.
They can nag and annoy you,
When you have been bad, they put you up for trial.

Above all, mothers are there when you need them,
They can be your greatest friends.
Put up with their tales and sayings,
Then they will be there until the end!

Holly Adams (12)

Fear

I am afraid of everything,
Films, illusions and ghosts that are haunting,
Are these things real or are they in my head?
I think about the worst ones when I'm in bed,
It goes on like a switch,
When the light goes off, I start to twitch,
As I slowly start to get into bed, all these thoughts come
Flooding into my head,
In my bed I lay still,
In my head the murderer goes in for the kill,
People call me silly, a baby and more,
But what I'm scared of is that I won't see the age of 24,
What will I think of tomorrow night?
Funny how everything changes with a flicker of a light,
I know now that none of it is real,
Now I'm not scared, I'm as hard as steel.

Alex Whitelock (13)

I Am

I am the pen that ran out of ink,
I am the brain that cannot think.
I am the garden full of weeds,
I am the book that no one reads.
I am the pizza that's never been eaten,
I am the girl that always gets beaten.

Carina Roff (14)

New Zealand

Homesickness is a terrible feeling
Loneliness and depression
Photos, heirlooms, memories
Remembering becomes obsession.

I left it behind when I was young
My family, friends and home
I set out to a new country
A new place for me to roam.

Excitement was eventually overcome
By incredible hollowness
The sadness showed upon my face
My mood so full of distress.

My trip back home was most enjoyable
Fun in every way
Thought it would not be the same
If I went home to stay.

Even now I've started again
Made a fresh new start
I always know that there will be
A place for home, next to my heart.

Rachel Lamb (13)

Friends

My friend is kind and thoughtful
She is trustworthy and pretty
Most people think I'm weird
She doesn't
I love my friend
She's the best
She never laughs at me
Except today
She did today
Cos she has someone else
Her new best friend
She's OK
I suppose
But now I feel alone
And now she never talks to me
And so I feel sad
So I found someone new
And she's OK
She's funny, loud and chatty
But I'll never forget
My old best friend
And how we used to be.

Emma Flewitt (12)

Jim

We have this very special friend,
We hope our friendship will never end.
We've known each other quite a while,
So now we know each other's smile.
We have had some laughs as we know
And over the years we've loved you so.

You have always treated us like your own,
Over the past as we have known.
You don't know how much you mean to me,
We hope through the past it's been easy to see.
We will always have the odd little cry,
No matter how hard we will try.

You are a man, who we dearly miss,
We wish we could give you a huge hug and kiss.
We've always wished things did not change,
Because not seeing you opposite is so strange.
To us, you're like a shining star,
Looking after us from afar.

You have always made us very proud,
We're sorry we've said it aloud.
You were always thoughtful, loving and kind,
Not that we even need to remind.
The cards you have sent over the years,
Have always made us shed a few tears.

We don't know what we did to deserve someone so great,
Love Leanne and Kayleigh, your loving mates.

Leanne Goldsbury (12)

Life Cycle Of A Mother

Age 5: I love Mum, she tucks me in on cold nights,
Whispers, 'I love you,' and turns out the lights.
Age 10: I don't mind Mum, she's OK, she's kind of embarrassing,
In a funny way.
Age 15: I hate Mum, she drives me mad!
She won't let me go out with that gorgeous lad!
Age 20: I don't mind Mum, she's OK, she was really embarrassing,
As I moved out today.
Age 25: I love Mum, she's passed away, up above,
As I tucked myself in, I whispered, 'Mother, it's you I love.'
Age 30: I miss my mum, got married yesterday,
And there's a baby on the way.
Age 35: I tucked her in, it's cold tonight,
'I love you,' I whispered and turned off the light.
Age 40: I made a fool of myself, it was quite funny,
I hope she isn't embarrassed of her mummy.
Age 45: She met a new lad, I think his name's Tony,
I won't let her meet up with him, he might be a phoney.
Age 50: She moved out today, I was so sad,
I was in hysterics, she must think I'm mad.
Age 55: I'm looking down on her, my baby, my honeybun,
Mother's life cycle, let's hope she's a good one!

Coco Stephens (13)

My Lost Love

As I sit here writing this poem,
I imagine a person sitting beside me.
This is no ordinary person though,
It's a beautiful young, caring girl,
A girl sweet, kind and gentle.

She would come round just to talk,
And as she does I sit there,
Sit there gazing into her eyes,
Loving eyes which sparkle like diamonds,
And warm my soul like no other could.

We would talk of days past and to come,
Laughing and joking together.
But I no longer take heed of her words,
Just the soothing tone of her voice,
A voice that is softer than falling snow.

As we sit and lie side by side,
I'd gently caress her soft hair,
So soft it feels like soft, smooth silk,
With its gentle, smooth texture,
And a sweet fragrance of perfumes.

Who am I to deserve someone so dear?
It's then I sit up, awake to reality.
Saddened of what is here, nothing.
I turn to lie again and weep,
Knowing she is gone, no longer in my life.

I know now I'm destined,
Destined to be alone and weep.
Weep into my cold, lonesome hands.
With a broken heart and soul alone,
Now all alone and weeping in silence.

Neal Shakespeare-Walker (16)

Mrs Brown

I tread so carefully as my feet, blue with cold dissolve right into
The navy carpet of someone's bedroom
The curtains are multicoloured and so thin when the decided bolts of
Heat and light seep through to colour the room a morning hue
A freshly-washed quilt is disguised as white snow, so gentle in its
Encasement, unsensed, unknowing in its touch

Beats of particular Sunday music are saturating the western wall, as
A long curved body is strewn diagonally within the bed
The soft white drapery horizontally hugs her,
Slung out near the carpet in a night's worth of stirring, chasing the
Illusive comfort
The mid-morning life of below hums through, and in the heavy-handed
Breeze of this April doors are slammed to provoke mild stirring here
And there
The objects in the room seem to run; the oil in which my eyes paint this
Scene fades to crown this vision of the sleeper

A CD player sends some moody song into the picture in time with
Each forgotten breath
Her auburn hair, thrown across her face, is hidden from me,
The spectator
The poet who trembles in this presence
For in waking she won't realise what ideas wrap her
Love is a cliché but even so,
This morning song is for the one who knows one million clichés
I would send if it were all an effort to inform someone that I loved her
The bed is low and the room is bright and Sunday and the whole world
Could not be even a few inches further away from here
I'm listening to her breathing still
I remain and she does not wake.

Sara Brown

Closest Person To My Heart

This person means the world to me,
Some say they are close to him,
Others say - who is he?

Who is this person you may say?
Do I know him?
Does he live down the bay?
No I say.

He lives in the best of places,
Miami, Hawaii, Florida?
No I say!

He is close to me in everyday life.
I talk to him when I can.
He's there through my troubles and strife.

His book is the greatest of non-fiction.
His son was a miracle maker.
Have you guessed this guy's name?

His names are numerous,
But;
I know him as *God*.

John Shipston (12)

I Miss You

It's a shame that we're over, it's a shame we didn't last,
But I'm going to try and forget you and leave it all in the past.

I wish we could be like before and everything would be the same,
So I wouldn't feel like this and go through so much pain.

I think about the times we had together and the things we used to share,
I wonder if you feel the same, do you even care?

I always think, what went wrong; I always think what changed,
I always think by hurting me, what have you gained?

I don't know what to believe, what's the truth and what's a lie?
I can't do anything except sit here and cry.

I look out of my window and think about us, do I have any more
Feelings left? Do I have any more trust?

I want to go back in time so I can be with you, I don't know
What to do because
I miss you!

Aysha Iqbal (16)

Birdsong

She sits at the kitchen table, crying.
She brushes my hand away
When I offer it, and
All I can hear is birdsong.

Suzannah Evans (14)

Prized Possessions

They don't sit up on the mantelpiece rotting away,
They stay with me forever and come where I may.

They remind me of the times I've had, precious as gold
They help me make new decisions based on the old
They are something to keep me happy,
To reminisce about.

Just thinking about them,
Stir up the emotions I felt at that time,
They manage to delete the bad ones
To resurrect my mind

I meet so many people,
And move on throughout my life.
I have so many good times
But what would be the point,
If I could not remember them,
What use would they be then?

They don't sit up on the mantelpiece rotting away,
They stay with me forever, they are my memories.

Maria Ward (13)

My Cat Saffie

My pussycat's my favourite thing,
I love her more than anything,
She will go out in the day,
Cos Saffie my cat, just loves to play.
She stays with my baby cat Tillie,
Even though she's so silly,
They stick together through, thick and thin,
That's probably because they're next of kin.
One quiet night, not long ago,
Saf didn't come in, where did she go?
Tillie sat and cried all night,
Waiting for Saffie to come into sight.
My family were very worried,
If they heard a noise off they scurried,
Cos everyone was by the door,
Just in case it was Saffie they saw.
We all went to sleep worried that night,
Thinking Saffie was in a fight,
Our cats come in, when it's dark,
I bet she was playing down the park.
Ten past six on Saturday morn,
It's as if Saffie was reborn.
She jumped the fence as fast as poss,
I wish I could tell her I'm her boss.
Dad brought her up to my room,
My heart was thumping, *boom, boom, boom.*
I was so happy to see my cat,
I doubt I will ever forget that.

Kelly Snow (14)

Mikey

Mikey is many things to me,
He's a partner in crime,
He's someone who I can't help but fancy,
He's my mate.
Mikey, there when I need to talk and need support,
He's kind and caring like most people but with one difference,
He's my best mate.
Mikey isn't perfect,
He has problems of his own and he isn't the cleverest on Earth,
But to me he's the greatest,
He's courageous and daring, not at all like me,
That's why I look up to Mikey
And sometimes wish I were more like him,
You could say he's my role model,
He's my best mate,
I love him to pieces, I wouldn't change him for the world,
I have great respect for Mikey,
He's done a lot in his time, most he'd rather forget,
He protects me from bad things he's done and in the world,
Because he's my best mate.
I love him,
Mikey's very brave to cope with his ordeals, and he gives me courage,
I really do appreciate him,
Mikey is the best person around,
He's loving and loves me,
He's always been there and I hope always will be,
He's my best mate.

Sarah George (15)

Only One Thing To Say

Too many words to fit on to paper,
What can I say?
I could say I'm sorry,
I could say I never meant to hurt you,
I could say forgive me,
I could just go and on,
But there's only one thing to say,
That would make your pain go away,
So even though you are close to my heart,
I have to say . . .
Goodbye.

Laura Muirhead (14)

You

You are the only one,
You are my moon and sun,
You are the air I breathe,
You are the one I'd never leave.
You are my dark and light,
You are the most beautiful sight,
You have the scent of flowers,
You have many special powers.
You charm me to fall asleep,
You cuddle me when I weep,
You are my moon and sun,
You are the only one.
You!

Jessi Mai Barber (12)

While You Were Sleeping

While you were sleeping
bombs were dropped at night
families prayed for survival
and to live until it was light.

While you were sleeping
innocent people lost their lives
children lost their mothers
and husbands lost their wives.

While you were sleeping
a young orphan lost his arms
no longer will he write with them
or feel using his palms.

In the war the people suffered
throughout the night and day
but was it right to do this
and was the war the way?

But here in the UK
the only thing I cared for
was the safety of my family
and to protect them from the war.

They are all very dear to me
each in their own way.
They are my angels here on Earth
and I pray for them every day.

Ashleigh Du Cran (16)

Close To My Heart
The Legend Of Bhagat Singh

I feel close to him, but I've never met him.
I love him, though I've never met him.
I cry and cry to hear that he sacrificed his life for us.
I'm thankful that he showed us that we were special too.
I'm grateful that he showed us to fight for ourselves.
I feel special that people notice us now.
The legend of Bhagat Singh.

Bhagat Singh sacrificed his life for the Sikhs,
to show that we are special too because the English
were trying to make us follow their rules
when India wasn't even their country.
Bhagat was just 23 years old when he was hanged.

Simeran Ghataora (12)

Inside My Heart

Inside my heart it's full of memories,
It's full of tears and important ceremonies.
It may be minute, tiny or small,
But I don't care, I treasure them all!

One of my memories from far away,
The tears, the sadness is still at bay.
There are people, places, animals and things,
Some cheap bargains, some expensive rings!

Some of them love, some of them hate,
Some when I was seven, some when I was eight,
Some when I was little up till I am now,
Some being good, some having a row!

Kirsty Dalziel (12)

Colour Emotions

The colour purple
For the deepest, darkest secrets
Which are held inside me.

The colour blue
Is for the mysteries
That lies behind them.

The colour brown
Is for the soil and the earth
Where I'm free from the people
Around me.

The colour green
Is the natural living
Which makes me feel right at home.

The colour red
Is for danger
That lies before us.

The colour grey
Is for death
That we cause
With our greed and emotions.

Karen Brewster (15)

My Teddy

Placed on her bed
She hugs him lovingly
Her secrets he is told
Her skin he does hold

One not so special day
He is picked up from where he lay
Taken up stairs to a place so high it might touch the sky
Put in a box with other broken toys he doesn't know why

Many tears later he hears voices below
Then steps on the stairs and a small breeze does blow
Dust brushed off his fur, and that hug again
Invisible tears fall, as he is put back in her den

After some years a small cry he does hear
Then a little hand grabs his ear
Dribble slowly falls down his fur
When in the door something begins to stir

A large hand grasps him, pulls him away
Back to her bed, while the baby is taken out of the way
By her face he is held steady
A small voice says, 'You'll always be my teddy.'

Penny Booth (13)

Everything Around Me Fades And Disappears

The trees die down turning black,
Their leaves begin to fade.
Houses fall back,
The skyscrapers lean,
The window's beginning to crack.
The grass grows inwards instead of out,
The concrete begins to crack.
The sky moves up and the stars fall out
Like miniature bombs they fall.
People stop and drop dead
As they receive the invisible kiss of death.
The screams are deafening
The stares give away how people feel:
Terrified and alone.
The sky disappeared
But the clouds are still there
And torrential rain begins to pour
From the heights of Heaven it comes,
Washing away the rainbows and all the bright paint.
As the rain stops everything fades and all that is left
Is a mass of black space.
I stand in one spot stunned and petrified.
Then as I look around to my surprise
Out of the pools of black space begin to crawl the people.
I hold close to my heart
My family and friends
All run to my side
I'm ecstatic to see them alive,
And with them around me I don't even see
All of the destroyed beauty -
They are all beautiful to me.

Vicky Wilkinson (14)

Where Is My Dog Kiraa?

Kiraa, Kiraa
Where are you?
In your kennel, the park, the zoo.

It's been a month now,
I hope you're alright,
I've looked everywhere,
There's not a dog in sight.

I hoped you would come back,
Then I began to wonder,
My heart is so empty,
It pounds like thunder.

Please come back, I miss you.

Steven Bingham (13)

My Little Brother

My little brother,
he's as cheeky as can be.
His hair is like soft, dry sand
and his eyes are like the sea.

My little brother,
born when light was dim.
The following morning when I awoke
I first laid eyes on him.

Kimberley Gough (12)

Something Special

Dear George,

Thank you for the note.
Nice to know you still remember me
and that 12 years of memories still
means something.

Do you remember that party?
We were five, you persuaded me to run away
because we lost pass the parcel.
Do you remember our last day at primary?
Persuading me to climb the school roof?
The picture's still on my wall.
Do you remember that water fight?
After PE last term - both of us sitting on the grass
Watching the rainbows . . . you soaked me!

So   many   memories

Thank you for the note.
It was nice to catch up,
You didn't have much time while you were with Judy.
And now that's over.
What's that?
You love me? You? George?
And you always have?
Sorry George
I love the memories.
But I know you too well, it wouldn't work
You're only there half the time.
Those memories are special
But so is my heart.
Sorry George, it means a lot to me
I'd like to keep it whole.

Emma Leedham (15)

Gone

Big, fat butter toffees,
Ice-cold milk,
My favourite swinging garden chair,
Sitting on their laps,
Singing childish songs,
You never realise what you've got,
Until it's gone.

Their happy smiling faces,
The twinkle in their eyes,
The energetic play in the garden,
The sunny days together spent,
Smiling in the sun,
You never realise what you've got,
Until it's gone.

You never realise what you've got until it's gone,
And gone they have,
Long ago, but the pain is still fresh,
My days are no longer spent,
Smiling in the sun,
You never realise what you've got,
Until it's gone.

Cancer came and took them,
Foul and black and greedy,
Now in Heaven they do rest,
Far away from me,
But they will lay in my heart forever, for,
You never realise what you've got,
Until it's gone.

Lindsey Swift (13)

The War

Every day I wake, I hope, I stand
My life flowing like a stream
But that is just a dream.
Every day I wake, I hope, I stand
That the world could go at least
One day without a bang!

Kimberley Simpson

Animals

Horses gallop as fast as a racing car,
Dogs bark, like loud banging music,
Cats laze around, like a sleeping baby,
A leopard runs, like an Olympic runner,
Rabbits hop around, like little children on their sports day,
A chameleon camouflages, like men and women in the army,
A hedgehog is as spiky, like some stinging nettles,
They should all be treated equally
As they are all part of our living world.

Jade Joanne Allen (12)

Guardian Angel

There is beauty in my heart, which doesn't always shine through.
But my faith is true and I have faith in you.

I am the one who will guide you through your day,
I will make sure you get through life okay.
For I am the one who discerns your secret fears,
As I am the one who has passed with you through all the years.

All the times you see,
Rest assured I will be with thee.
When your heart is low
I guide and you follow,
And I will show you the path to take,
When you are down
And when you heart aches.

You are the one who is always there,
Always an ear and always will care.

I will do my best through each passing day
To bathe you in light and help you find your way.

Kaylee Knox (15)

Everything's Changed

He meant the world to me.
I loved him so much.
He never left my side.

Why was I so stupid?
I had to leave him there.
Why did I forget?

Now he's in a better place, I hope.
Looking down on me.
Now he's taking care of me.

I try not to cry when I think about him.
It's so hard.
I try to keep a brave face.

Nothing will ever be the same again.
Everything has changed.
Nothing can replace him.

I miss him so much.
The cuddles were so comforting.
I miss my blue ted.

Rosie Grindrod (14)

My Little Tammy Fur

As I sit down,
On the comfy chair,
She comes to me,
And purrs away.

I stroke my hand,
Across her hair,
So she sings,
A little prayer.

She puts her head across my arm,
My goosebumps disappear,
Her fur like silk
And smells of milk.

I love her so,
She's always
My little Tammy Fur.

Yalinie Sivapalan (12)

Zero G

From *Four Feather Falls* to *The Secret Service*
Your puppet shows gave me pleasure.
They've given my family and I so much fun;
Something we will always treasure.

The heroes of your shows were rather square,
Like Steve Zodiac and Troy Tempest,
But there was always someone fun lurking in the background
I liked Phones the best.

The bad guys tried to conquer the world:
Masterspy, Titan, The Hood,
Captain Black, El Hudat, whoever it was,
In the end, evil lost to good.

Along the way you treated us to explosions,
Exciting submarines, super cars,
But best of all were the high-tech spaceships
So we could conquer the stars.

'Anything can happen in the next half hour'
Said Stingray's Commander Shore.
After seeing your shows, we believed it could
And we'd always watch again for more.

So it's for all this, Gerry Anderson, that I thank you now,
For giving us not only great TV,
But also for giving us so many memories
And it's these that are FAB.

Alice Crane (14)

Moments

My heart longs for the day when courage reigns.
My purpose longs for the time when love stains.
My hands long for the touch that banishes pain,
When peace colours the lives of all who blame.

My tears yearn for the words of a gentle voice.
My eyes yearn for the chance to rediscover choice.
My skin yearns for the opportunity to rejoice,
Over the entrusted youth but forgotten noise.

My lungs pray for the night when we can breathe.
My soul prays for the season to conceive.
My life waits for the fortune to believe,
In the hopes men have about their want to retrieve.

And when I step back and look upon the world that is,
I realise that it will never be mine but always his.

Kayleigh Miles (16)

Gone

One day he was there, the next he was gone,
Leaving us to feel all alone,
In our hearts there's an empty space from where his love used to lay
Our memories are good, none are bad.
When he left we were sad,
Thinking about him every day,
Thinking of the times we used to play,
He's gone now but I know,
That he's up there looking down from the sky above.

Charlotte Hemstritch (14)

March

I looked up at the heart-shaped balloon
Wandering in the pale March sky.
It shimmered scarlet-silver
As it danced around the golden pie.

My child wondered who let go
Of such a special gift,
As my hair shone scarlet
In the cold.

I did.
I let it go
Many years ago, to fly
Go,
To taint the sky
No longer burn my red eyes.

Its shape grey thin,
Helium was down,
It grew some creases
Like tiny dark frowns.

It hid behind the naked trees
She followed it as it went
It did glow
Like a full moon
But it disappeared,
Like a flame from a match
In the wind.

My heart-shaped balloon
Was hers,
To lose.

Selina Ulhaq (16)

I Like, I Love, I Do

My friends, my fans, my family
They all mean so very much to me
I love them all with all my heart
I hope nothing will make us part

I love to play a lovely sport
Called tennis on a tennis court
This takes place every Saturday
I have such fun in many ways

I listen to garage, R&B and hip hop
The hip hop makes you pop and drop
The garage makes you shank a lot
And the R&B is spicy hot

I like to go ice-skating when I can
I love to play a tune on a steel pan
I like to go on missions with my friends
I love going to the funfair till the session ends

So now half my life has already been told
There's still much more that will unfold.
I'm living my life the way it's been told
I'm getting older so you better behold.

Natasha Merrifield (14)

Because She Is My Mother

If it weren't for her
I wouldn't be here,
Writing this poem right now.
When I'm upset
She makes me happy,
I often wonder how.

All the cleaning and washing
She does every day,
Finishing off with a sweet-smelling spray.
Picking me up
Sometimes from school,
I value her presence like a crown jewel.

The luxuriousness
Of her evening meals,
It's better than any other.
She's joyful, playful
A bundle of fun,
Because she is my mother.

Toks Dada (13)

For Mum

You never seem to know
How much I care
And how I would miss you
If you weren't there

When I'm mad and I shout
You think I don't love
But the truth is that I'm
Just a girl growing up

I need some space
And give me time
And your little girl
Will begin to shine

This poem is for
My special little star
Who showed me the light
When things were so dark

I thank you so much
For being with me
And even if I don't show it
I'm grateful for things

Mum, this poem is dedicated to you
In these few words I hope you see
How much I love and thank you
For being my mum and there for me.

Sarah Morris (13)

My Cat

She lies,
she crawls,
curled up on the end of my bed.
Her purrs fill the empty night
sleeps soundly till the morning light.

She plays,
she eats,
prowling silently.
Her damp, pink nose
is like a rose,
the prettiest one I know.

Emily Cleaver (12)

Close To My Heart

Close to my heart
I hold this thing tight
For fear that it might break.

Close to my heart
I hold this thing tight
Hoping that I can keep it forever

Close to my heart
I hold this thing tight
My most beloved teddy bear!

Laura Newton (12)

Grandma

This poem I will dedicate,
To a dear friend that I lost,
I called her Grandma since I was two,
Grandma, I loved visiting you.

You sat me on your lap one day,
And together the piano we did play,
You read me stories, played with me,
This is how it used to be.

Christmas morning I'll never forget,
When I opened my pressies from Santa,
I sat with wrapping paper everywhere,
We visited you at Christmas every year.

You smiled as you watched us open our presents,
Me and lil' sis Emma,
You were always smiley when we came to stay,
Whatever the dilemma.

As we grew older, so did you,
Living by yourself because much harder too,
You moved into a home, so you were right nearby,
To start with we just did not understand why.

We drew you pictures for your walls,
And made you pretty cards,
Then one day we did not go,
You'd gone to Heaven, Mum told us so.

We were older then Dad explained it all,
No more pictures did we draw for your wall,
But Grandma you were close to my heart,
I cried when we were pulled apart.

I miss you still, even today,
I wish you were here so we could still play.

Alice Neve (15)

My Family

My family,
They live with me,
Play with me,
Come and see.

How much have I learned by copying them?
How to walk, eat and talk I have learned from them,
I will share this everlasting gift with my pen.

I go on holidays with them,
Have grown up with them,
They are the creme de la creme.

Where would I be,
If they left me alone?
I'd be on the streets without a home.

When I leave home I'll see them less,
But home, that's where they'll be,
My brilliant, brilliant family.

I could roll around with superlatives,
But at the end of the day I'd be nowhere,
Without my family.

Jonathan Pilborough (13)

A Photo Of Stars

On my bedside table is a photo,
The frame is made of silver,
It sparkles and shines,
I polish it every day
And keep it locked in a secret box.

On my bedside table is a photo,
Forget silver! The frame's made of solid gold,
It glitters and glistens,
I scrub it every day,
I keep it locked in a box with a thousand bolts.

On my bedside table is a photo,
And I swear the frame is made of diamonds.
They shimmer like crystals,
I take each one out and rub it clean.
I keep it locked in a cupboard with a giant padlock.

On my bedside table is a photo,
The frame is made of stars.
They zoom around the photo like rockets.
I never touch it so it stays perfect.
I keep it in the tallest tower of a castle like a fairy-tale princess.

On my bedside table is a photo,
The frame is made of plastic, not silver, gold, diamonds or stars.
But the photo's made of all of them.
The smiles are silver, the features are gold,
The clothes are diamond and the memories are made of stars.

On the bedside table is a photo,
Four people standing arm in arm.
A snapshot of precious memories.
A picture of a true friendship, that's slowly fading,
So I keep it locked within a poem.

Sarah Taylor-McAllister (12)

You Are The Only One For Me

I think I'm in love,
You're as sweet as a dove.

You're always on my mind,
People like you are hard to find.
I feel alone when you're not there,
We truly make the perfect pair.
I am so lucky to have you,
I hope you love me too.

I think I'm in love,
You're as sweet as a dove.

You are the only one for me,
You make my heart fill with glee.
You make shivers run down my spine,
Just to think you are mine.
I adore your cheeky smiles,
I feel like leaping a thousand miles.

I think I'm in love,
You're as sweet as a dove.

I am proud to be your girlfriend,
I promise our hearts will never have to mend.
This poem I hope you'll treasure,
And when you read it, you'll fill with pleasure.
This poem was written just for you,
All the words that it contains are true.

I think I'm in love,
You're as sweet as a dove.

Lauren Jane Matthews (11)

The Piano

Scant days before my birth, you were bought -
We arrived the same date, you and I.
You form my first memory, the day Great Aunt taught
me middle C; your echoing, trembling sound,
with her wrinkled smile towering on high
and my feet hanging far from the ground.

Years later, when we heard she'd moved on
it was to you I turned, and through the empty house
rang the soft notes of my dirge; on and on and on
as I played out my grief; Christmas Day I woke
the house with carols and amongst the holly and the gold
we sang as the pale dawn broke.

Every day for twelve years I ran my hands
over your keys, rising and falling like a wave;
then the hard times sent you and I to separate lands.
But still each night I find you again,
deep-sleep playing all the tunes in my head.
I know your every whorl of wood and ripple of each note,
as you knew my every feeling, played instead of said.
One day I'll play you again, but until the day of that find,
like a soundtrack to my life your music plays in my mind.

Tessa Baker (15)

Music

The sounds echo through my mind,
Surges, quivers.
Endless rhythms beat upon me,
Take control.
Each note sharp and clear,
Yet soft.
Freer than the air I breathe
It whispers to me.
Play on!
Never stop -
The very sounds elevate from the soils of the earth.
Time stops.
The trees sway and bend to my command.
The air is full, and then . . .
Silence.

Victoria Duggan (15)

The Day I Met You

(Dedicated to Dan)

I never thought luck was a friend of mine
Always thought it to be a waste of time
Well - until the day I met you.

Just when I thought the wind would blow me away,
And when I thought my dreams had all faded away,
You came and lit up the road ahead -
I don't know what to say that I haven't already said
But I'll never forget the day I met you.

I know I don't always appear to be grateful
In fact I'm usually sulky and hateful
But without you I'd be less than a smudge on a page
And filled with nothing but hate and rage,
So it's just as well I met you.

I never believed in true love
Never thought dreams would come true
Oh how I was proved wrong,
The day I stumbled upon you.

You are the oxygen feeding my flames
You are the strength lifting these chains
You are the comfort keeping me sane
You are the hero who reduced my pain
You are the one that made life bearable
You are the protector of all that's terrible
I love you
From the depths of my heart and soul, I do.
I was nothing until the day I met you.

Caroline Watson (16)

God

Ultimate power, ultimate strength,
The one I look to again and again,
Guiding star, shining light,
That burns piercingly through the night,
Above the clouds, above the sky,
'Over the rainbow way up high,'
Far as he is, seems so close,
Surrounding my body, wrapped like a cloak,
Next to my heart, next to my brain,
His sadness is the earthly rain,
His cosmic dance in the Heaven,
Are the Earth's worldly movements seven:
Stars light, plants grow,
Animals live, rivers flow,
Winds gust, land spreads,
The eternal Earth ever spins.

Piriyenga Mahendrarasa (15)

Joined At The Hip

(Dedicated to Danielle Ramsden)

We're there for each other
Through thick and thin
And in races and games
I let her win.

I give her hugs
I buy her sweets
And cinemas and swimming pools
Are some places we meet.

We are inseparable
Joined at the hip
And if we weren't
My heart would rip.

I lend her my tops
She does the same
And we laugh at my jokes
Even though they are lame!

We'll be there for each other
No matter what
And we'll be best friends forever
For eternity, full stop!

Kelly Summers (12)

Nan

Nans are everywhere you look,
Nans are there for you,
But I know if I looked everywhere,
None would be like you!

You are always there for me Nan,
No matter what I say or do,
And incase there's any doubt,
I love you!

It was different as a small child,
I didn't understand,
Then I made a great discovery,
Nans are there to give a helping hand!

You're always there for me Nan,
Supporting me in what I do,
I guess this is my opportunity to say,
I'll always be there for you!

I don't know how I cope without you Nan,
I don't know what I'd do,
You're like my second mother Nan,
I love you!

Sarah Oates (13)

Close To My Heart

Close to my heart
A family's there
Nannas and grandads
That always care

Aunties and uncles
Mum and Dad
Because they're there
I'll always be glad

Timmy and Tommy
I love very much
They are my budgies
And soft to touch

I don't know what I'd do
Without cuddly toys
I love them much better
Than the boys

Now I've told you
What's close to my heart
If you liked it
Go right back to the start.

Naomi Roberts (12)

My Hamster Molly

I look back at the days,
But now it's all a haze,
As Molly did depart
And it tore my heart,
As we filled her grave,
These memories
I shall save until the end of time.

These days, a bad dream or so it seems,
Molly, yes she's in my dreams,
These memories will not abate,
I no longer can concentrate,
My body full of regret,
I cannot let it take over my life.

Yet I won't forget this,
As my despair walks into the abyss,
Back to work, another day,
On the boat at the bay,
What's in stake and lies on,
As I drift into the horizon
Molly will always be there in my heart.

Benjamin Smith (12)

Darkness

Darkness.
I yearn for light, yet...
Only darkness.

I sit and wait
Wait and dream...
You never come.

I see your face smiling
Come closer! I cannot reach
Then...gone.

Just as a sunset is snatched behind a hill,
You cloud my vision with beauty
Then vanish.

Never again can the sky be filled with you.
New light tries to fill the void - breathtaking to the untrained eye.
Me? Nothing.

No photo or film can capture you
No painting or words.
In my mind and heart you dwell.

Let my mouth brush yours
Let me feel life pulse through you again
Embrace me.

Darkness.
I yearn for light, yet...
Only darkness.

Charlotte Wright (14)

For Grandpa

Why didn't you say goodbye, why did you leave?
Why have you closed your eyes and forgotten me?
There was so much I still wanted to say,
Why didn't time stop before you were on your way?

Where are you Grandpa, where have you gone?
I have tried to find you all night long.
Are you dancing in Heaven, with angels of white,
Or sleeping peacefully under imperial light?

Do you miss me Grandpa, like I miss you?
Are you watching over me like they say you do?
Can you hear me Grandpa, I'm calling out to you,
But I know I'll never hear you, whatever I do.

Grandpa, you own a very special place in my heart,
And nothing will ever change that, no matter how far we are apart.
I know one day you'll take me by the hand
And lead me over a bridge of stars, to a new land.

Xiao Ou Li (13)

Me And You

Here I am, I'm thinking of you
And all the nice days we've been through
Your friendship was the nicest gift you gave me
I will never forget it believe me
I'll keep this friendship safe in my heart
And never will we part

Never have you let me wear a frown
And I have never felt down
A great cheering up you have always done for me
And I can always come to you if I ever worry
I can always be there for you too
And I will help you make it through

Nice and helpful, that's who you are
And for me you are a star
Funny and good humoured you are too
And a great deal of laughing we always do
You are special in every way
That's how you'll stay

Very brief this message will be
But I hope it will mean as much to you as it does to me
I never told you
But I really love you
And I hope this friendship lasts forever
Like the dying and blooming of a flower.

Valérie Giner (12)

Close To My Heart: My Dog Shuffle

Shuffle
Every morning when I come down for breakfast,
You're always there to greet me.

Shuffle
When I'm depressed or angry,
You always have a way of making me feel better.

Shuffle
Whatever you're doing,
You don't mind me scratching you behind the ear.

Shuffle
You bark at the most ordinary things,
I don't mind, I think it's your individuality.

Shuffle
You always dream of chasing squirrels,
Making twitching movements and barking in your sleep.

Shuffle
You'll be my friend forever,
I'll never forget you, and I'll always miss you.

Shuffle
You're all anyone could want in a friend,
You run with me in the park and always seem to make me smile.

Ross McDowall (12)

So Little Of You

So little memory of which I can make sense of,
So little clues to the missing piece of my heart
So little links to help to find you again
So many problems to keep us apart

So little photos to construct a vision
So little time to discover your path
So little hope to see your face in the crowd
So many dreams to be shattered in half

Every day I look at the faces in the crowd;
And wonder if that's where you are
Every day I look at the photo in my drawer;
And hope that you're not too far

So little evidence to prove you're well
So little keys to unlock hidden doors
So little signals to point the way
So many soul-bruises and sores.

So little opportunities to say hello
So little chances to hold your hand
So little luck to share your wisdom
So many people each a different brand

Every day I look at my family tree;
And realise your face is not there
Every day I wish upon a star
For your help for your heart to repair

So close to my spirit yet so far from my terrain
The mysterious missing member, whose departure causes my pain.

Lyndsay Hall (14)

Close To My Heart

He knows my every move, and every thought I think
He knows when I cough or sneeze or blink.

He's inside my head every second, every day
And listens to my words when I pray.

He knows what makes me laugh and cry
Even though He lives above in the sky.

He sees everything I see through my eyes
He knows my secrets, my thoughts, my lies.

He hears what I hear through my ears
If it's his voice, her voice, He feels my tears.

He feels my pain and sadness too
And wonders with me what to do.

He tastes what I taste on my tongue
Sweet and sour, He knows what I've done.

He smells what I smell through my nose
And walks with me on my toes.

He laughs and smiles and hopes with me
Of a life together for eternity.

Me and him, we're two different parts
But He's the one I keep close to my heart.

Siân Roberts (16)

Close To My Heart

I look out of the window and look up to the sky,
and I can see that twinkle in his eye,
I can see him smiling down at me,
with that cheeky laugh, *tee-hee-hee!*
I think to myself and wonder why,
he had to go and leave my side?
I can't stop crying, I can't take the pain,
knowing you won't ever be back again!

You said I'd always be your little girl,
I thought that would last forever,
but you left me in this grown up world,
I had to pull myself together!
At the end of the day, you showed me the way,
I'm never in doubt, someone's watching over me!
When you're flying way up high,
show me your love
and you can be my angel for life!

Gemma Swinford (14)

Let Me Show My Love For You

Let me show my love for you,
In fact in several ways.
I'll love you until the end of time,
You are my pearl of ultimate shine,
You are my raison d'être,
My pièce de resistance,
And through those dark and dreary days,
You would always know how to change
My frown
When I was down
My love for you in many ways,
Ad infinitum.

Gavin Shiel (13)

Love Poem

I love thee my beloved,
in so many ways.
I will cherish thee always,
in all my living days.
From when I awake in the morning,
to watching the stars at night.
I will love thee, for eternity,
with passion and with might.
Even when I'm grieving,
laughing and smiling too.
I shall love thee always,
and hope my love is true.
My love is pure and from the heart,
my love will shine on, even after we part.

Amy Curry (13)

Love Poem

Cry me a river, drowning in my tears
I will hold you close, fight away your fears
When you are all alone, sitting in your chair
I am soft and fluffy, your little teddy bear.
Let me tell you a story, I am an open book
When you are hungry, I will be your cook
I would walk on water, just to be with you
Cross over the seas, just to be true
I am Cupid shooting you with love
Flying the clouds above, I can be your dove
Now that you're around, my broken heart has healed
Speaking to me lovingly, my lips are truly sealed
When your life has ended, and you pass away
I will still love you more day after day.

Georgia Crawford (13)

How I Love You So

How I love you so, like the morning breeze,
How I love you so, like the earth beneath the tree,
How I love you so, like the shimmer of the sea,
How I love you so, like the song of a buzzing bee,
How I love you so, like the sweetness of toffee,
How I love you so, like the strength in coffee,
How I love you so, like the sun shining bright,
How I love you so, like the shining moon at night
And if you love me too,
Give me the reason.

Catherine Brady (13)

Love

If I can be your bee
Then I'll make you my honey
Let me be your money pot
I'll bring you lots of money.
Your hair is dark, your eyes are brown
When we're apart I feel I frown
Don't care what it takes
Let me be yours.

Let me be your scarf
On those snowy winter days
Let me be your daydreams
When you want to drift away
If I die this very day
Let me be with you in many ways
Don't care what you say
I'm sure I'll be yours.

Amy Duff (12)

Appreciation

The sun beats down on a dusty street,
A handmade football comes flying past,
The boys are happy,
They've had their meal,
Mum managed to find something for them to eat.

The rain falls down on the soft, warm floor,
Two complaining children come rushing past,
The boys are angry,
They've had their meal,
But that's not enough, they want more.

Up before dawn, glad to be alive,
Mama sends them off to work,
The walk is long,
But the boys don't complain,
The hardest part happens when they arrive.

Woken up at eight to the smell of cooking,
The boys angrily march downstairs,
They have it all,
But they don't care,
They can't see further than where they are looking.

Different lives, worlds apart.

Some people,
Appreciate the little they've got,
Some people,
Want more though they have a lot.

So when you think that life is unfair,
Take a look around, things will always be there,
To show you that people will always care,

To show you how lucky you are.

Nicola Horne (13)

My Cat

I love my cat
Her coat is so warm
She sleeps on a red mat
Two years ago
Is when she was born

Her fur is soft silk
She likes a pat
She loves her milk
And I love my cat.

Richard Habergham (13)

Teams

My team is like a sisterly crew,
You help them and they'll help you.
We have parties and pranks and fun galore
Oh no! My friends are never a bore.

We shout and we scream, we fall out of course,
Vicki once said that I smelt like a horse.
Just because my scent was likened to an equine
Does not mean we do not get on fine.

We giggle and gossip and text on our phones,
We listen and understand when somebody moans.
We're groovy as gravy and really funky,
At the end of the day we're all cheeky monkeys!

Hannah Quinton (12)

My Soldier . . . A Memory

A blink,
In that split second of exposure,
My brain is startled by,
The choking black smoke,
The lit up grey sky,
Only to find,
It's another day that won't be too kind.

All in our uniform,
Lined up at the ready,
No time for dreaming,
Of being at home with my teddy,
Charge!
The starting gun fires,
As we run into battle,
No slacking when we run through the mires.

Close to the city which is now all ablaze,
From bombs dropped that night in an aeroplane faze,
My boots full of water and a gun on my back,
We rush to the trenches with no time to slack.

The first gunshot is heard,
Rattling through the air,
A sudden silence brings ringing to my ears,
Then my heart sinks as I hear a groan like a bear,
I hate to think,
That there's bloodshed already,
And hope to God,
That the next dead's not me.

Olivia Faire (13)

Freddy

When I'm all alone,
When the pain gets too tough.
When I want to scream and moan,
When my life is too rough.
I think of you Freddy,
Then I'm right as rain.

You're soft as a feather,
White as the new snow.
Smelling as sweet as a heather,
I'd cry if you were to go.
I've known you forever,
Though time doesn't matter.

In the spring as the wind wails,
And the blossom blows into my face.
My love for you never fails,
Pretty like the white lace.
You're always there when I need you,
You're Freddy the teddy too.
You're the first to touch my heart,
The one I love, never to be apart.

Emily Baxter (12)

My Grandparents

My grandparents are always there for me,
Always making endless cups of tea.
I never get bored when I go round,
There's always something new we've found.

The weather's always fine and bright,
We plan our outings in the middle of the night.
Then we go to church, which is great,
I've now made lots of new mates.

They shake their tablecloth outside, and all the neighbours stare,
It's like an embarrassing nightmare!
When we go out of town,
We wind the car windows down!

I never ever want to leave their house,
I cry like a little timid mouse,
But I think of them every day,
I love my grandma and grandad, they're the best in every single way!

Clare Shortman (13)

Rugby

R   ough and tumble
U   gly to watch
G   ather for a line-out
B   rilliant tackle
Y   ell of my team when they score.

Thomas Armes (11)

He's Getting Too Old For A Little Sister

He was always there for me, the big guy watching out for me.
He made me laugh, he made me cry, especially when he hit my eye.
When I was small and he was tall we got along quite well.
He'd tell me stories of fairies and trolls
And later on he'd mess up my dolls.

Our holidays were always fun,
We'd play all day in the boiling hot sun
We always had a splash in the pool trying to keep ourselves cool.
When I got tired at Disney World
He carried me round and showed me the sights.
When I went on the fast rides he would be there making me secure
On the ride that I had to endure.
He always liked to make a joke, he was quite my special bloke.

As we grew older our bond started to break,
He was more interested in girls and dates,
We still had fun, just not as much
And even though he's in the room next door
I felt like we lived on a different floor.

When he started kissing the girls
I'd be sat there thinking I'm going to hurl.
No longer the only girl in his life but second best
After the girl he met last night.
This sort of thing left me feeling weird
Seeing my spotty brother with a girl near his beard.

On the day that he finally had to leave
I couldn't find it in myself to believe.
My big bro gone, vanished in a puff of exhaust.
The car drove off, it sped away,
Returning with only the driver the next day.
The rest of the day I spent moping around,
The house felt so quiet without his usual riot.
I missed him so much.

Only after he left our house and it's become quiet like a mouse,
Have we really noticed how much we miss him.

And when he comes back and eats all the food it's nice to see him
For about two days until he gets on our nerves again.
Then you start praying for school to start
But then I miss him all over again . . .

Lucinda Taylor (13)

Love

Love I can see in her sparkling eyes.
Believe me this sort of love never dies.
Instead it waits and lies
In the darkness of her heart,
Then it flies like a lark being set free,
To the open world with glee
And onto that special *he* it lands
And is locked firmly with tight hands.

Amy Ward (13)

My Friends

My friends are like my family,
Always there to cheer me up,
To dance and play happily.

To share secrets and giggle,
Have sleepovers and shop,
Play around in class and fiddle.

My friends will stick with me forever,
Through good and bad,
Whatever the weather.

So when I'm feeling down,
Something has gone wrong,
I don't worry because I remember
My friends are always around.

Abbey Charley (12)

Love

Love is strange, it's so confusing,
When you look back it's quite amusing.
One moment you're in, the other you're out,
It makes you wonder what it's all about.

You never know if it's really for you,
From your very first kiss to saying, 'I do'.
If you're going to become a husband or wife,
It's one thing that lasts you all your life.

I know for a fact that it's the best,
It gives you time to play and rest.
If it's from your friends or from a lover,
The first person to love you is always your mother.

Eleanor Trounce (13)

Memories

Time is a twisting twister,
Going round and round,
Spinning faster and faster until I have to *stop!*
Feelings are writhing
The nausea is getting to my head,
But there's only one thing that's stopping me from going crazy,
Memories!
The summer heat beating down on my head,
Sand between my toes,
A whiff of fresh cut grass,
An autumn walk down a dusty path,
And all these things are the closest to my heart.

Jessica Knights (12)

Digger!

When I was born she was there,
watching over with a beady-eyed stare.
Always wearing the same coat,
white and brown, calm and sound.
She would follow anyone around.

If you were ill she was there to care,
sickness and pain were things she would share.
Someone to cuddle, who was always there.
She would take to anyone like a friend.
Love is a thing she could always lend.

She saw a lot of our others pass,
Jess, Boots and a few more, buried under the grass.
On a walk she could really run,
when worn out she'd ride with Mum.
But, if raining, she never did come!

Now she's gone never to come back,
up the silver, gold and diamond track.
I really do miss her, if you knew her you would too.
Gone for only a year and of her love I starve.
Digger was the best dog I ever did have.

Tim Walker (12)

Mitre Peak New Zealand

A clear blue sea
White mountain tops behind
Captures you like iced wind

Pure green forests
A dream sight for dreamers
Mountains play with clouds

The snow still falls
Mitre peak stands taller
The water doesn't move

Pebbles shimmer
No houses are in sight
No one at all is here

Small fish flicker in the water
Wild animals roam round the fjord
A natural kingdom.

Paddy Uniacke (12)

Icon

As he walked through the door
My heart sank to the floor
I wanted what I couldn't get
'Cause another girl he had met.
Nobody will ever know
How I used to love him so.
His jet-black hair and dark brown eyes
I hate it when he nearly dies.
My heart nearly burst when that bus exploded
I can't wait for *Matrix Reloaded*.

Maddy Ball (12)

Close To My Heart

Here you are close to my heart
with me every day,
your love pinpoints me with a dart
straight and true all the way.

I could not live without you for one single day
in life, maybe in death,
I'll be with you all the way
till your, and my last breath.

Cheeks all rosy
hair fiery-red,
just looking at you makes me feel cosy
you'll be the same till I'm dead.

As I said from the start:
together we climbed life's rungs.
You're something close to my heart
my very own, my lungs.

Sam Weatherstone (12)

Roadrunner

His comb like a crown, triangles of red
coat a vibrant spectacle of colour
cranes his neck to crow
stands tall and proud
his strutting march brisk and purposeful
sudden charge to oversee a dutiful hen
fine flamenco dance, puts the harem hens in a trance
his precision eye and razor beak
cluck, cluck, cluck, to attract
the hens to a treat.

George Router (13)

Best Buddies

Someone or something important to me,
A memory or a picture maybe,
My father, aunty, cousin or mother,
My dog, my sister or my big brother,
But the ones who'll be there till my life ends,
Are all the kids who have become my friends,
There's a multitude of great people here,
Though to me, my friends are always most dear,
They all have a talent of their own sort,
Whether it's English, French, reading or sport,
Sometimes they are happy and prosperous,
Other times they can make an enormous loss,
This variety of all different children,
Come together to make an awful din,
But that doesn't matter - they're always there,
When I'm sad or being treated unfair,
Because they are my very best friends
And they will help me through life's twists and bends.

Jack Stevens (12)

Love

Love is a sweet and tender thing.
It makes us happy and joyful.
It also brings the two different sexes together
And wounds them when it breaks.
I love love because it fills me with joy
And brings happiness to my life.
I don't know where we would be without love,
Probably in fights and where we would have wars.
If I didn't have love
I would be dead,
Because, love is a harmony of nature.

Jamie Damerell (13)

My Bed

My bed is one of the closest things to me
Whether it were in a castle or a marquee
A good night's sleep is guaranteed

Its soft, fluffy pillows that you sink into
That lovely feeling is untrue
When you're in, you stick like paper and glue

The soft sheets you lay on top
Your body hits the springs in a drop
As you run and bellyflop on top

Bed as smooth as a water skin
Go and lay and get tucked in
Then get to sleep with a wide grin.

Jacob Taylor (13)

Close To My Heart

I carelessly fling my dirty clothes on the floor
And walk out my room shutting the door,
5 minutes pass and I walk back in
And all my clothes are put in the bin.

Soon after they are taken down the stairs,
Of this good deed I wasn't aware,
Who put them in the washing machine?
To make my clothes nice and clean?

It wasn't my dad,
It wasn't my sister,
It was the person close to my heart . . .
My mum.

Katie Shingfield (12)

Summer Evenings

Evening bells ring across the marshes,
As the sun starts to set,
Nightfall is coming, but not quite yet,
As badgers come out for their night stroll
And bunnies go into their holes.

The sky is filled with lots of colours,
Purples, pinks and the rest of the bright sun,
People have gone in, pleased with what they've done,
While shops are shutting, no time left to buy,
And one little insect has come to die.

The air becomes rather cold,
Bats are around, flapping about,
The sky turns dark, and stars shine out,
It's no longer a special summer's day,
Tomorrow - who knows? It could rain.

Rozzi Clarke (13)

Teams

When you do PE are you the first they pick?
When you do PE are you person who is always 'sick'?

Do you brag and boast that you're the best,
Or are you the person who fails every test?

If you think, it does not matter
There's no 'I' in team or it will shatter.

So try your best in every team
And you will come out with a beam.

Paul Lake (12)

My Dog

Black bouncing bundle of fun,
With wobbling legs and frantic tail,
Follows me with ungainly run,
Great loyalty that will never fail.

Full-grown now, sleek with noble head,
Sniffs the air, eyes bright awaits my call,
Trained to the gun, gentle carrier of the dead,
Never fails to find where they fall.

Grey muzzled head lifts to greet
Homecomings,
Not able to run or jump,
Now plods beside me down the street,
Sees my gun, tail gives a gentle thump.
His collar now hangs behind the door,
Fond memories stay for evermore.

Chris Aldous (13)

West Ham United

West Ham wear claret and blue,
We stick together just like glue,
Premiership or Division One or even Division Two,
We will still stick like glue.

We are now in Division One,
So we will kick Norwich City's bum,
Even though we are down in the blues,
We will be back and you won't have a clue.

We will be back,
So you lot should start to pack,
They are so great
And I will support them to their fate.

The Hammers' fans will start to sing,
From the minute the season begins.

Josh Jaggard (12)

Wilkinson My Hero

Who kicks like him
I wish I could
L ong and straight between the posts
K icks so lightly but oh so true
I wish I could
N o one can do it quite like him
S oaring into touch
O ver all our heads
N ow we're almost there

Makes his mark before he kicks
Y es, yes, yes, the crowd all roar

H ave we time to convert the try
E ven though the time is close
R eady, steady, here he comes
O ver the posts and we have won!

Clement Juby (12)

Unlocking The Door

A door is hard to open without a precious key,
Each golden one is hidden within the heart of me,
They're entwined in my body and so difficult to find,
It is only my loved ones who know how to read my mind.
And every single thought which passes through my head,
I have so many memories of special things they've said,
When days and weeks pass and they are not there,
My life seems meaningless, fruitless and bare.
I know that they will not be with me forever,
But we must enjoy moments that we share together.

Emma Griffiths (13)

Ten Things I Hate About You!

I hate the way you smile
I hate the way you're so vile
The way you treat us wrong
That's why we want you gone.
You never teach us wrong from right
That's why we always fight.
I hate the way you haunt us with your bad jokes
I hate the way you crumble all our hopes.
(We wanna thank you for all the pain you've caused
Cos we never wanted to know what Hell was like of course.)
I hate the way you take the mick
You make us all think we're thick.

So here's to the person,
No names, but you know who you are
And you really need to change, as you're the worst by far.

Libby Lake (12)

I Wish . . .

I wish I was a celebrity, in glossy magazines,
always getting complimented on my stylish clothes.
I wish I was a singer, my albums in the charts,
my songs being on the radio, always being played.
I wish I was married to one of the Liverpool players,
sitting in the stadium cheering the team on.
I wish people would talk about me and say how trendy I can be,
being told I am so pretty and gorgeous and lucky to be who I am.
But maybe I don't want to be in the press all the time,
maybe it's OK to be ... just me!
So all these wishes should stop,
and I should be pleased to be who I am and who knows
perhaps all these wishes might one day come true ... I wish!

Beth Loaker (11)

The Cat

Once, a mangy, smelly cat came into my garden.
I absolutely hated it.
Black and white it was, except the white was grey with dirt.
That day I hated it.

Once, a mangy, smelly cat came into my garden.
The same one as before.
It looked at me with its eyes, like crystal balls they were.
That day I disliked it.

Once, a mangy, smelly cat came into my garden.
The same one as before.
It purred at me and rubbed around my leg.
That day I liked it.

Once, a mangy, smelly cat came into my garden.
The same one as before.
I smiled and walked towards it, picked it up and stroked it.
That day I loved it.

Robert Horwood (12)

The Band

I love to play my electric guitar,
I play along bar by bar.
When I start to play,
I get transported away
From this world
To the pearled gates of paradise.
Then the drums kick in,
They make such a din.
So I play louder,
My plectrum is turning to powder.
But the drums are still there,
They sound like a bear.
So I play faster,
Please say it won't be a disaster!
And I shout, 'Faster, faster!'
The bass kicks in,
Smoothing in that din,
I hope it won't go down the bin.
We are all playing fast,
The sound is travelling vast.
Suddenly it stops.
It is over.
I return to Earth on the cliffs of Dover.

Peter Lockett (11)

A Special Gift

The gift that I dream for is not posh clothes,
It isn't a wide-screen TV with a top of the range VCR that I crave for.
It isn't a brand new game that I want,
It isn't knowledge or a 1st prize winner that I love.
The thing that I want,
The special gift,
Is love itself.

Isaac Shortman (11)

The Little Boy Who Stood And Stared

I saw it standing there,
Then I realised it was a bear,
I couldn't run,
I found out I could only stand and stare.
Why, oh why didn't I run?
It was only a little bit of fun.
Now I'm gone,
No one cares.
I was only the boy who stood and stared,
Most thought I was weird
And had a world of my own.
Then they found out, I had no home.
They all laughed at me,
Especially when I sneezed.
They didn't care about me.
They all ignored me as I walked down the street.
They all knew that I was ill, as I was as white as a sheet.
So when I went to the woods for food,
It was my destiny to find that bear,
Be killed viciously by that bear.
Not many cared,
As none of them knew me,
Because I was the little boy who stood and stared …

Luke Smith

Snow

Snow
Sets me aglow
With
Anticipation
Of
Fun to be had
Because it's so rad
Snowboards and skis
Swoosh through the trees
Edges and curves
Beginners to swerve
They've lost their nerve!
Jumps and big glides
Fall and you'll slide
But it's fun when you ride
The wind in your hair
Get a big air
Land if you dare
Try to look cool
Impress the whole school
Fall, you're a fool.

Will Maddocks (13)

The Ways I Feel About You

I love the way you smile at me,
I love the way we talk,
I love the way you always act,
I love the way we walk.

I love the way you never care,
Or worry loads about
The way you look or your hair,
Makes my heart turn inside out.

I love the way, when you smile,
Your whole face crinkles up,
I love the way you light my day
And finish with a touch.

I love the way just you and me
Talk so close together,
Cos when we laugh I feel
That you and me will be forever.

I hate the way you kick the tins
And you play the fool,
You always have this great big grin
And think that you're looking cool.

I hate the way we always fight,
I hate the way we argue,
I hate the way I believe I might
Have this feeling of love for you.

I hate the way you kiss me,
Though I always kiss you back,
I hate that something in your kiss,
That something that you lack.

I hate the way round your fingers I'm wound,
I hate it that you lie,
I hate it that you get me down
And the way you make me cry . . .

Charlie Pullum (12)

Close To My Heart Is School

My school days are an occupation
　　They lie very close to my heart
Where learning is fun together
　　To give you a start in life.

At infant school starts the cycle
　　With words displayed on the walls
Where teachers and staff are so friendly
　　If you try you'll earn praise from them all.

At junior school the work gets harder
　　In class you'll use textbooks and sheets
Maths and English homework is set
　　To be returned the following week.

At high school there are clubs galore
　　Cricket and football to name a few I like
New subjects include PSHE and IT
　　And SATs are vital tests in Year 9.

Soon there are exams and coursework to contend with
　　The Year 11s face a torrid time
Good results are required to enter the sixth form
　　Good results are required to succeed in life.

With university comes independence
　　And efforts beyond your best
Late nights become a frequent occurrence
　　To gain the top mark in a test.

The final exams are a nightmare
　　But the effect on you is the same
A degree or masters 'you've done it'
　　Bringing your education to a bright, jubilant end!

Aidan Brown (13)

My Family

My dad, what a good lad,
My mum, she used to have a big tum,
My sister, she is like an annoying blister,
My granny, she never had a nanny,
My pappy, he's a good little laddie,
My uncles, what a bunch of smuncles,
My cousins once removed, they were soothed,
Last but not least,
My cousins, they come in dozens.

Joseph Petzold (12)

Untitled

At 12, life is wonderful,
It is like a gift of no other comparison,
Thrills are common and friends fickle,
Depending on how you treat them.

Thrills come in many ways,
For instance skateboarding and surfing upon a bay,
That would be my choice,
But not even one of these things
Would match having a friend.

I myself board away from home,
Pleasure and unhappiness often kick in,
But the best bit is probably going home,
Into that dome of love and care.

Soon I will be thirteen
And I hope that this will not change,
As my life continues,
But I hope it stays wonderful.

Robert Lowton (12)

Misty

I have many things that are special to me,
One of which is my dog, Misty.
When she was small she slept by my bed,
You could hear snoring from her tiny head.
I really like taking her for walks,
Sometimes I think, *oh why can't she talk?*
If she could, she'd be a really good mate,
Not that she isn't already just great!

Rory Morgan (13)

Pets

Pets come in all shapes and sizes
You can buy them in a box or win them as prizes
Pets are usually man's best friend
But sometimes, the rules they bend
They can poop on your grass
And sometimes chase cars
They can chew on your shoe
Or drink water from the loo

But my pets are always very good
Whenever I come calling
They come rushing up for food
They never come up in the night
And check up all around
They never make a horrid noise
You cannot hear a sound
They don't have any annoying claws or habits
That's because my pets are rabbits!

Christian Thorley (12)

My Cats

Small black cat, neat as a pin,
Sharp emerald eyes, full of sin.
White bib, white whiskers, socks like snow,
Secretive Socks, where do you go,
When you're not lying in the sun?

Gentle Sooty, black as night,
Eyes like saucers, bold and bright.
Ambush keen, mysterious stare,
Meander past him if you dare,
When he's full of fun.

Darting here and leaping there,
Unseen adversaries in the air.
Mercurial nature, gentle paw,
Feline fury, settles a score.
My cats are second to none.

Chris Barraclough (12)

She

She struts through the school with a glint in her eye,
People flock round her, though Heaven knows why.

She wears hoards of jewellery and high-heeled shoes,
Just to be different, and break all the rules.

She's pretty, she's glamorous, but that's only skin deep,
For under the surface, a monster does creep.

Her words are like silk they flow like a river,
But do not be fooled, her tongue is a killer.

Her charm is her weapon, her beauty her tool,
Which she uses to beguile, a poor lost fool.

I've seen through her mask, I know the real 'she',
And now to expose her, for all to see!

Kate Revell (13)

I Hate Poetry

Poetry is pointless,
It's boring and useless,
I hate it so much,
As I don't have that poetic touch,
Whoever invented it,
Was a complete and utter twit.

I'm getting bored,
I wish I were a lord,
For when you are mighty and tall,
You can do stuff all,
I'd love to do sport instead,
Because at this rate I'll soon be dead.

Ah, I'm on verse three,
This means I'll soon be free,
From this dreaded thing,
And I really did try to get it rhyming,
I must write no more,
As it is against my law.

Now I'll bring to your head,
What I've already said,
You may say it's late,
But if there's one thing I hate,
It's poetry!

James Pearson (13)

The Colours Of My Heart

A pretty picture,
A magical dream,
A distant vision,
A breathtaking scene.

A mark of trade,
In a far-off land,
A promise given,
From his own hand.

A burst of colours
For which no one could pay,
A mixture of rain
And the sunshine's ray.

Gold is looked for,
High and low,
But a pot is found
Beneath a rainbow!

Rachel Mannings (12)

My Dog

He's cute, he's furry,
He's white and black,
When he jumps up, he's blurry,
Like a jumping jack.

He looks like a puppy,
With his smiling, grinning face,
His tail long and fluffy,
Wagging at a pace.

The reason that he is so close to my heart,
The thing that sets him and all others apart,
Is that he cheers me up when I'm feeling down,
Sitting there, with that face, what a clown!

Alexander Mitchell-Hynd (13)

My Dog

My dog, strange animals dogs,
Active, cuddly, fussy but sometimes aggressive,
Watch her chase her long tail,
But all those longs hours, she just fails.

This is my dog, what do you think?
Don't just stand there, give her a wink,
What do you think she likes? Pink,
Try and reach her over a radio link.

Tom MacCormick (13)

Prep Time

The stuffle and huffle as disorganised students rush to get books
The agitated remarks of stressed-out teachers trying to regain order
The reverberating clang of bells resounding, nearly always late
The silence, broken only by the odd snuffle, whisper or cough
The wave of calm that washes gently over the entire room, as bodies
                                        settle and minds start to whirr
The rhythmic beats from a personal stereo turned up too loud
The rustle of a note, full of secrets, passed unstealthily and the girlish
        giggle of the receiver, as they relish secret, scribbled sentences
The graffitied desks, worn from years of work and wear
The clashing colours of the unaesthetic curtains
The frantic sign waving, for use of equipment that was long ago lost
The frustrated faces of children who 'can't do it'
The flicking and yawning of the bored
The watery glare of flickering, strip lighting
And an array of heads working hard for those deadlines

This is prep time.

Alice Finch (13)

A Special Someone

I love the way you kiss my lips
I love it when you smile
I love the way you speak to me
I've loved you for a while
I love the way you laugh with me
Not many people mind
I love the way you're there for me
And how you've been so kind.

Steve Williams (12)

Teams United

Can you live without your teams,
Be alone and sad,
No one to work with,
No one to win with?
I know I really can't.

I'm part of my rounders and family team,
My friends and school too,
We laugh together,
Play together
And think together too.

If I was without my loving teams,
I would be boring and sad,
But because I made a commitment,
People like me, for who I am.

I'm glad I have my family team,
To look after and care for me,
But most of all, I'm there for them
And we can be a team.

Victoria Smith (12)

My Family Team

Could you live without your parents,
Feed and care for yourself?
You need your team, your family,
Your friends and other people.

If you didn't have your team,
You wouldn't win,
You wouldn't laugh,
You would be alone and sad.

I'm glad I'm in the rounders team,
I'm glad I've got my family team,
Because if I didn't, I'd be boring,
But because I made an effort,
I have my friends and family.

Alice Dring (12)

Teams

November 11th 1918 the guns roar
Both teams in extra time there's no score
Then silence, silence . . . sweet as a bird
Teams 1st, 2nd, now there's a 3rd
3rd is the 2 teams joined together
Hopefully harmony forever
Iraq vs America, England too
(Hang on, this is not right)
For men in teams, to fight through the night
A man dies next to you, he is your mate
The gun fire goes like drums in the deep
And slowly the animals creep
To the place of peace. They are a team
And in my dream
I see the team of the earth
Joined from death to birth.

Tom Maddocks

Kibble Football Team

K   ick-off starts the final
I   n every player there's a star
B   oot every ball in the goal
B   oys pass and throw
L   ooking for an open goal
E   xcited players and fans scream and shout,
    when the players in black come running out.

F   oul is called
O   ne shot with the ball
O   n target we shoot
T   op right goal and the
B   all is in the net
A   nd all salute
L   ucky we are that everything went well
L   eague winner's cup we become and everyone yells.

T   rophy is ours we hold it up high
E   ach person in the team
A   chieves their dream
M   anagers are pleased
    when the Kibble boys come out to tease.

Scott Watson (15)

Kibble

K   ick-off starts, the ball is in the net
I   'm in glory but the keeper's upset.
B   ack to the changing rooms and everything's swell
B   ack on the pitch, everything's hell!
L   et's get back on track to win the game and get defeat
E   veryone in the team is on their feet
    to hold the cup and show our defeat.

Levi Riley (15)

Untitled

Here I am, standing amongst a crowd,
I speak but no one listens, should I shout out loud?
But instead, I don't even make a sound,
Sometimes I feel like going to a high
And throwing myself to the ground.

I don't think they like me because sometimes they don't even look,
I think they just ignore me and treat me like some invisible book,
When will they listen, when will they care?
And when will they stop thinking that I'm not really there?

I think everybody is special
And everybody should be treated as equal people.

Keiran Sneddon

My Homeland

Through the trees which tell a story
Of a place that I once knew,
Not a forest, but a jungle
Full of mist and dew.

On the hills and over mountains
Lie this country's signs of life,
People who stay together
Throughout any pain and strife.

Mankind and endless animal species
Roam this plentiful land,
Woman and her child learning about the many creatures
Together, hand in hand.

From barren desert, lush jungle
Or the heart of Bogota,
This is the country, my homeland
Special *Colombia!*

Claire Bradley (14)

Close To My Heart

You're so close to me, you're almost a part of me.
You're so close to me, you can read my mind -
Tell me what I'm thinking.
You're so close to me, I'd be lost without you.

You're so close to me, I want to feel your heartbeat constantly,
Even when we're thousands of miles apart.
You're so close to me, I can't ever let you go,
Where you go, I long to be.

You're so close to me, I'll have you by my side forever,
You're so close to me, you understand me.
You're so close to me, you know everything about me,
Things I'm sure I don't even know.

You're so close to me, you're there to guide me.
You're so close to me, you're always there to give advice.
You're so close to me, your thoughts conjoin with mine.
You're so close to me, parts of your life are my life.

You look after me and encourage me,
You keep me safe and inspire me for life,
Who are you?
You know.

I will keep you within me always.
Whisper your name when I am lonely and when you are not there.
I know somehow you'll always be near.
For you are,
    so close,
        to my heart.

Carla Plasberg-Hill (14)

My Family

My family is so close to my heart,
I wish that we will never part,
For if they were to leave my sight,
I'm sure I'd live a life of fright.

My family love me for who I am,
They will not change me even if they can,
We have a special bond of love,
That is as pure as a snow-white dove.

Laughter fills our house each day,
This is what I have to say,
We have a very strong relation,
Which is surely part of God's creation.

They help me out when I am sad,
My loving mum, brother, sister and dad,
Even when I have done wrong,
There is a place I will *always* belong . . .
With my family.

Never will I part,
From those so close to my heart.

Kavita Patel (11)

Rugby

Now there is a sport which makes my year worthwhile.
But for this sport you need skill and style.
In the scrum you need the strength of a lion,
As if you were made of nothing but iron.
To reach the rucks before your enemy or foe,
So at the end of the match you have things to show,
In the line-outs you need to be fierce and tall,
So when you leave you don't feel so small.

Now for the backs, it is vital they're cunning and skilled,
So that when they're passing the ball is not spilled,
And they need skilful dummies, sidesteps and kicks,
They also need diving tackles and ankle flicks,
When the ball is kicked the fullback should catch,
Then shout 'mark' before they can snatch.

If you want to learn more, like distanced drop goals,
So the ball sails straight through the upright poles.
Tap-kicks are special when they're unprepared,
Because the enemy is shocked and mostly scared,
The sport is easier when you win all the mauls,
It helps your players withstand most the falls.
So I suggest practice training and matches,
Therefore perfecting cobwebbed patches,
But for this sport to be magical and good,
You should follow this guide, I wisely would.

William Howell

Bungee-Jumping

The closest I came to flying
was the day I thought I was dying.
400 feet and an elastic rope,
my heart was beating I was losing hope.

Today was to be my first bungee jump,
the thought making my head thump,
my mind was all over, I was in a whirl,
I didn't want to do it till I saw this girl.

Although I was scared with thoughts all over the place,
in front of this girl I didn't want to lose face,
as I jumped into the air my eyes started to glare
the ground was getting so near,
would the rope snap? My greatest fear.

Down and down I fell,
my God this is Heaven as well as being Hell,
at last it stopped and to my surprise,
instead of just hanging I started to rise.
I bounced up and down like a yo-yo on a string,
alone in my harness, to the rope I did cling.

Soon it was over
I heard the cheers of the men,
I climbed up the stairs
and did it again.

Steven Burke

A Friend Until The End

When I wrote this poem, it was not just on my behalf,
I wrote it from the Kibble boys and all members of the staff.
You never think it will happen to someone that you know,
You never think it is the last goodbye when you watch somebody go.
Gordon will be missed and I say that without doubt,
Living life for the day was what he was all about.
I know it will take time for our pain and hurt to mend.
So I say this on everyone's behalf
That Gordon was a friend until the end.

Ross Davidson

Kibble School

My football team is Hibernian,
They play in green and white,
I go and see them play
At day and at night.

We've had a bad season,
We all know the reason.
We've had problems with money, injuries and bans,
But no matter what, we Hibs fans
'We'll support you evermore and
We'll all cheer when the Hibees score.'

David Burns (15)

Close To My Heart

He leads me on my way to the path of light,
A unique figure creates my sight.
He wakes me up in the morning,
And sends me to sleep at night.
My senses were a gift from him,
That I should be so grateful.
Our life aim,
Is to succeed.
He teaches me to respect others,
As they would to me.
He's created every illness,
And every cure.
It's our job to help the human world,
With the knowledge he has given us.
Every step of our lives,
Is a longer step into eternity.
Our life aim,
Is to succeed.
Be the best that we can be.
In order to make him happy.
We should have him by our side,
Even when trust is lost.
We struggle to earn what we can,
Working hard has its reward.
In order for him to be pleased,
We should work hard and succeed.
He is God Almighty,
And I have all faith in him.

Shaima Najar (14)

Manchester Utd

M is for the might of United, the pride of United,
   the flight and consistency to win games.
A is for the United anthem always an encouraging song,
   bring the 'Glory Glory' home!
N is for the noise of the United fans,
   a big part of our success, the loud racket of encouragement
   always a special factor for the champions.
C is for the craftsmanship of the players,
   always a fascinating show with Ronaldo,
   Keane, Scholes and v Nistelrooy an absolute spectacle to watch.
H is for the hunger of United stars, the determination to win
   every match.
E is for exceptional expertise, a match can be turned around
   by a little show world class.
S is for speed of United, always a helping hand
   with the influential Ryan Giggs running up and down the flanks.
T is for the test United pose with every team in the running,
   week in, week out.
E is for excitement of Manchester, the emotional hunger to do well.
R is for Ruud v Nistelrooy a big, big part of our success last season.

U is for the unity of the champions, the original force of power.
T is for triumphant United always looking to achieve
   in whatever they do.
D is for the downfull of United, it may be far away but who knows?

Siva Orimolade (13)

My Days In Kibble

My first day in Kibble, it was a very scary day for me
So many new places and faces to see
Would they be friendly or would they want to fight
I already wished it was night

I went into my unit as quiet as a mouse
Hoping nobody would notice if I went to my house
Then I quickly realised it wasn't that bad as I thought it would be
Nobody really noticed or tried to bother me

I have been here nearly a year, never once have I felt any fear
I have done a lot better since I came to this school
My teachers no longer think I am a fool.

Shaun Kerr

Zola

Close to my heart is Zola.
Zola is a wonderful player.
36, well past his day
But is still determined to play.
His skill on the ball is tremendous.
His free kick is what made him famous.
He cares about others, not just himself
And that is why he is close to my heart.

He joined the club in '96
And still he tends to show
That after seven years
He is still fit and ready to go.
The Italian gives Chelsea that extra bit of class
He has scored at important times
So that is why he is close to my heart.

Daniel Heath (13)

Family

F   amily, always there for you,
A   nnoying, but it's true,
M   ums love you to pieces,
I   'll always remember the good things, never the bad,
L   ike you always love me, how could I repay you back?
Y   ou are like a dream that I never had.

Reshma Gohil (12)

Close To My Heart

I can't help but think about the times we've had together
We'd go out, have so much fun no matter what the weather.

There is no secret I have to tell that my friend doesn't know
She always knows how to cheer me up if I'm feeling low.

I hope one day, I'll get the chance to tell her how I feel
And how if ever she needs me I'll be right there, I will!

The way we'd laugh and play all day, has led me to believe
If you're feeling down or sad a friend is all you need.

We are so close, two peas in a pod, I'd hate it if we were to part
That is why, above all things, my friend is close to my heart.

Joely Clarke (13)

Close To My Heart

My mum is especially close to my heart,
She's been there for me right from the start,
She cares for me 24 hours a day,
Like a full-time job without any pay.

My dad is ever so close to my heart,
He's loving, caring and especially smart,
I care for him, he cares for me,
This is something that is quite easy to see.

My brothers are close to my heart,
Beating me up is their best art,
They may hit me here and there,
But, I always know they'll be there to care.

My grandfather is very close to me,
Even though you cannot see,
The man who died quite long ago,
The man who taught me, 'be good to your foe'.

Remember,
Being close to someone and loving them,
Is the best thing in the world.

Merkala Indrakumar (13)

Cars

Without them I'd be nothing, just another soul,
Searching for the one, the only one.

The one that turns you on!
The one that catches your eye.

The one that you adore,
The one that you dream of driving.

For me it's the F50,
A Ferrari that is, top of the range.

A top speed of 202mph,
550bhp with G-force acceleration.

A bit of a rip-off, but it's worth it,
At £380,000, it's not cheap.

But it's worth the pleasure,
The V12 5.0 litre turbo engine,

Sitting behind you, purring away,
Until you get bored, then *roar*, goes the engine.

The power makes you become ecstatic and excited,
The exhilaration of accelerating to 60mph in 3 seconds.

I want one. I need one. I have to have one.
I've been saving since I was 3 years old.

And I can only just about afford to get one of the alloys!

Daven Raithatha (13)

Something Close To My Heart

There is something close to my heart,
the bodyshell is more like a great work of art.

It takes a lot of skill to drive it
and it costs a lot of money to buy it.

I'm still working on my driving,
at the minute it seems to be flying.

I am still developing new techniques
but in the end it does all come down to driving and timing.

I don't want to find a new hobby
I am extremely happy where I am.

At the minute I am on top of the competition
the only thing that might make me leave
is the price of staying in the game.

David Kinman (13)

Close To My Heart

Friends are the family we choose for ourselves,
If only we had the same simple cells.

Sometimes we fight, sometimes we argue,
I wish it is all simple to get through.

But it's no good, no it's never simple,
There is always something wrong.

We just try our hardest to love one another,
That's why the human race goes on.

Ian Smart (12)

Friends

We tell our secrets
And share our dreams
We gossip and chat
We are as one team.

Friends are our family
We can never let them go
Holding them to the heart
We really love them so.

You can approach them with ease
They will never let you down
You can tell them anything
They will never make a sound.

Friends are always there
Standing nearby
Waiting for you patiently
With a shoulder to cry.

They would offer almost everything
Sacrifice all they had
Telling you jokes to make you laugh
To make you happy from sad.

Friends are a trophy, a prized possession,
We hold them close with all our pride
By being trustworthy and loyal
They will stick by your side ... always!

Aarabi Thavendrarajah (13)

My Friend

I have lots of friends,
But there's one who's always there,
There to help me out,
When I can't cope,
She was there to give me hope

Without her I wouldn't be
Where I am today,
I've known her most of my life,
Since reception
When we were only four

People used to say we looked
Exactly the same
Every teacher
We had got mixed up
With our names

But then there came a day
Where I had to go away
And leave my school to move to a new place
Which is where I am today,
So here we are now, far and far away ...

We are here today,
Both separate from each other
She was one of my best friends
And still is one of mine today ...

Priya Parmar (13)

Close To My Heart

Close to my heart lies within
A memory of a dear old thing.
Memories of days full of fun
As you lay looking up at the sun.
But now sadly passed away
In our hearts you will stay.
But still remembered every day
Now you have gone away.
We will still love you anyway
17 years we have all shared with you
And my, what a lovely dog you were too.

Gemma Thompson (12)

Calling Out Her Name

She fell off a tree as a flower at fall,
Her smile so happy as the sunset and sunshine,
Her soul as sweet as chocolate,
Her as pure as gold ...
She was once in my heart and now always will,
We stepped into the world together,
But will leave holding on tight!
Most of all her love was warm.
She blossomed with pretty petals,
An angel sent from Heaven,
A best friend sent for me,
It was a very special gift; she was the best part of it ...
Through the years she grew lovelier ...
Her petals expanded, her roots remained!
She faded away, was blown far away,
But came back with a gentle breeze,
My call for her ...

Dina Jachi (13)

Close To My Heart

Looking back on where we first met
I was so in love
That I cannot forget
I knew you were the one
That person in my life ...
Close to my heart.

First day of school ...
Not a glance my way
But still, all I did was drool ...
To make matters worse
You walked right past
To Miss Popular ... Mandy Lurse.

I thought to myself
Why? Why
Is it always the pretty girls?
All they do is lie ...
Then ... a miracle
You walked my way.

You said
'Hey look ... boohoo!
New girl has toilet paper stuck in her shoe.'
As you walked away I looked down
Dreading what I would see
Aaaahhhh!

It was just a dream ...

Krisha Patel (13)

The Charm Bracelet

I know it may seem silly
but this thing is very special
It's gold with tiny gold objects dangling from its chain
A golden dice, a golden leaf, a golden this, a golden that
Yes, you might have guessed it
Yes, it is a golden charm!
Why is it so special?
Through thick and thin
this lucky charm is always there
My charm bracelet helps me through those dreadful nightmares
which then might I add, becomes my dreams.

Laxhmi Soneji (13)

Untitled

The world spins as my life shreds,
Everyone is so caught up in their problems
They don't see how everyone else ends.
Don't look at others, just think of yourself
For it might turn on you,
The world never ends.

Problems come,
Problems go,
The sooner they come,
The faster they go,
One a little problem here,
One bigger problem there,
You'll soon see
They're everywhere.

Iris Pitta (13)

A Gift From Above

No one could be
As thankful as we.
To be blessed
With the very best.

A mother who cares
And is always there.
To share a tear
And rid every fear.

A father who smiles
All the while.
Through good times and bad,
Making us laugh when we're mad.

We want you to know
That we love you so.
You're precious in every way,
We thank God each day.

Even though time may do us part,
You will forever reside in our hearts.
Wishing you a very happy anniversary with love,
To the most cherished gift sent from above.

Pinky Nari (17)

Untitled

I may not be a poet at heart,
But maybe a storyteller.
It's my dream to write, some day soon,
A wicked and grand bestseller.

For what, so far, I have accomplished,
I send my thanks to you,
My mother, teacher, friends of course,
For helping parts to come true.

Urging, urging for me to write
More of my developing tale.
Reading and suggesting improvements;
Without you I'd definitely fail.

Thanks to you, I've been able to write
This poem now that you read.
I hope you receive the message I send
For your kind and loving deed.

Thanks again and again once more
To my mother, teacher and chums.
It's down to you that I've managed to write
And soon hopefully true will my dream become.

Michelle Birks (16)

Close To My Heart

You were close to my heart,
affected the way I looked
talked,
thought.
I trusted you with all I had -
my deepest secrets
and all the tales.
My memories of you
live on in my mind
play with my heart.
They take the happy song
and change its tune.

You were close to my heart.
You held it in your hand
like a piece of glass,
as if a single fissure could damage me
forever.

Katy Campbell (15)

Loved Ones

My grandma is great
And I love her so much that I ate
Everything she cooked for me.
I was even told that when I was young
I would not let anyone sit on her lap.

My grandad is brilliant,
He used to give me chocolate after every meal.
I used to kneel
With him to do a bit of gardening.

I used to like to bring my dinosaurs with me
And both my grandparents would play along with me.
My grandma would sing to me
When it was time for bed,

> *'You are my sunshine*
> *My only sunshine,*
> *You make me happy*
> *When skies are grey,*
> *You never know dear*
> *How much I love you*
> *Please don't take my sunshine away'.*

I would drift away
To dreamland and sleep hollow,
Dreams would follow
Of my dear grandparents,
My so near grandparents,
My so dear grandparents,
My grandparents.

Alex Juriansz (12)

Lorrain (Pottery Doll)

She's always waiting there for me
When I get back
She stands there quite content
With her fur coat and accessories
Her eyes are the most beautiful ones you've ever seen
As well as her long golden hair
She's always ready to listen
Even though I know she's not real
To me she's my best mate.

Suzanne Kimberley (14)

World

Colours streak like graceful leviathans
Making the air shimmer with its sheer beauty
Stars wink at the gazer far below,
Who watches them shine in the endless void,
Clouds swirl above the drifting continents,
With oceans and seas spilling between them,
Birds sore high overhead,
Singing to the beauty of a new dawn,
A breeze rustles through the trees,
As I think to myself, *Earth,*
This is my world,
This is my home.

Nicholas-James Haslam (14)

Close To My Heart

You're close to my heart
I dream about you every day, I miss you so much
The way you were funny and made me laugh
I hoped that the day when you had to leave would never come
But it did and now you have made me regret not telling you
That you're close to my heart
You said it to me once, but I never believed you
And then when you said it the day before you left
I got a warm upsetting feeling knowing you would never say it again
So when the wind whispers to you
Hopefully my message got to you saying, *you're close to my heart.*

Wendy Gransbury (13)

My Precious Memory

(Dedicated to Reg Adsett)

Sitting here writing this poem, I think strongly about my grandad a lot,
I very clearly remember him still from when I slept in a cot.
Even though he has been dead nearly six years, I still shed many tears,
I talk to him when I'm all alone about my thoughts my fears,
Or feeling happy or sad,
After I've talked to him I feel really glad,
That my loving memory of him will never fade,
Through him my life has been made.

Louise Wilson (11)

Friends

Friends are funny
They are kind and nice
They can be big or small
They should always be there for you.

Friends will believe you
Never hurt you
Never laugh when you fall
Never steal from you.

Debbie Southern (11)

Music

The voice lights the spark within
To strive for that perfection.
Like a hurricane it buffets and regales
Setting you soaring through the moment
So good it has to be a sin
Beats like a temptation.
Bass reflecting your attitude,
Freeing the spirit of the muse.
Inhibitions to swoon under the weight
Of the freedom within a disc.
An air guitar interlude,
The soul has been set loose.
Not on any planet
Closer to a heaven.
The voice in expression
To set all tension free.
Move as guided by the heart
Nearest thing to liberation.

Jessica Sandy (15)

My Little Golden Locket

I have a little golden locket
I've had it since I was born
I got it from my gran and grandad
They're not here anymore
Sometimes I really miss them
I just wish they could come back
Even if it was just for a day
But when I really miss them
Do you know what I do?
I take my little golden locket
And put it close, close to my little golden heart
Where gran and grandad will always stay.

Charlotte Leaf (12)

Close To My Heart

What is closest to my heart?
It would have to be my brother.
He is small and excitable,
Chubby and character full.
When I walk in after school,
He sits in his high chair
With a mouthful of drool.
He has chubby legs
With a round smiley face.
The worries of my day have gone without a trace.
Now no one will take the smile off my face.
It seems so amazing in what seems like just a few weeks
He has grown up so strong with loud laughter and shrieks.
His name is George I have to say
That I never thought I would feel this way.

Sam Wood (11)

Close To My Heart

Life can be hard, it's not always fun
But as the darker times come, let me be your sun
It's not every friendship that lasts this long
But the days spent together just make ours more strong
Together we've been through some very rough times
And I'll try and stick by you through the more that arrive
So many memories stay preserved 'til the end
You'll stay close to my heart as our friendship transcends.

Helena Wittenbach (13)

World's Best Mate

When I'm crying, feeling down
When my smile turns to a frown
You'll be ready to dry the tears
And wash away my lonely fears
I've had boyfriends, quite a few
You were there when they came unglued
When I feel I need you most
You are there not trying to boast
How my dates all went wrong
I haven't really known you that long
But you are never going to fade away
Never leaving me, you're here to stay
You're my best friend, totally cool
Even though I can be a fool
You've stuck by me, you're so great
A round of applause for the world's best mate.

Vicki Lewis (12)

Gareth Gates

At London Arena I saw Gareth Gates,
My mum said it was okay to take some mates.
He looked really smart all in white,
I was screaming and smiling with delight.

I was singing and dancing all through the show,
I was that close to him - in the front row.
I love his smile and spiky hair,
I blew him a kiss - I didn't care.

I like his looks, songs and voice,
He could be my boyfriend - *what a choice!*

Nadene Kennedy (11)

Vulcan

Vulcan was a loving dog
He had a kind heart
Vulcan was a faithful pet
He guarded the house at night.

Vulcan let me hold his paw
And cuddle him when I was sad
He was as fluffy as a teddy
And as brave as a bear.

Vulcan was seven-years-old
A German Shepherd in fact
Although he isn't with me anymore
He lives on in my heart.

Loren Turner (11)

I Have A Memory

I have a memory
In the back of my mind
Of a pet
Who was always so kind.

She would snuggle up to me
And lick my feet,
And if I was eating
She would try and eat my sweets.

My dog was always so nice
Because I loved her so,
But now I don't know where she is
Because we had to let her go.

We had to give her away
To someone my nanny knew,
We had to because her skin was bad
And it made my brother sneeze, *achoo!*

It was all a very long time ago
But she could still be alive,
I doubt that very much now
But I hope she lived the life she survived.

Now I have a pet rabbit
I love him all the same,
But I do miss Lady
And calling her name.

And I hope history won't repeat
Because I would like to keep our family rabbit forever,
Well with me anyway
So we can stay together.

Cassie Crompton (13)

Badger

There are several things close to my heart,
My mum and dad, those for a start.
My brothers and relatives, our rabbits and hamster,
Our cats, Sid, Tobi, Ollie and Jasper.
But, from this list, I choose Badger.

Our 'Baby Badger' came to us with Jasper.
From an evil feral, Badger turned softer,
Into a dribbling, purring softy,
As lovable and friendly as can be.
But, why did he have to die?

His soft, chunky, black body, white bib and toes,
What was the reason he changed? Nobody knows.
His cute, chubby face and clumsy appearance,
Inspecting himself in the mirror, he's the cat everybody wants.
He loved his food and adored our company.

Pick him up, he'd hang on your arm,
Every morning he was my alarm.
Jump on the bed and dribble on your face,
Wait for you to clear a space,
Curl up purring and fall asleep.

But, alas, he disappeared, never again seen alive.
Out for the day, and not there when we came back.
Two weeks or so passed,
A neighbour found him dead under their car, his death a mystery,
Our 'Baby Badger'; close to my heart.

Ashleigh Rouse (14)

Disaster In Love

The wild boy is like fire
Burning my heart
The ashes of youth continue to fall
Leaving me drifting in the wind

Mum's warnings were like ice
The boy's fire melted them away
There were no rings, she warned
To circle our love

Love has split my heart
I am a dying swan
In a sea of thought
Sinking.

Hannah Walkley (12)

I Can't Live Without . . .

I can't live without my mum and dad,
Not my brother 'cause he's always bad.
I can't live without food,
Or else I get in a bad mood!
I can't live without my mates,
Or else I would be counting one, two, eight.
I can't live without my stuff,
Oh! I forgot my pillow, which is full of fluff!
I can't live without my television,
Because my brother wants to watch Chucklevision.
The things I can't live without are everything!

Elaine Tsang (12)

Goodbye

Standing in his room
Staring at the space,
The space in which he once stood,
I see his pale white face.

Connected to machines,
Tubes all through his arms,
His eyes full of pain,
His sweaty body shaking with upturned palms.

I reached for his hand,
And squeezed it so tight,
He tried, he did, he tried,
To squeeze back with all his might.

I held him close,
I wasn't letting him go,
They told me he was getting better,
The doctors, they told me so.

But I knew I was losing him,
I couldn't bear the thought,
The colour from his face quickly drained,
Even though he was going, he fought.

He went so cold,
A machine started to beep,
Nurses ran in
And I started to weep.

Even though I've lost him, even though he's gone,
The pain is still there, carrying on and on.

As I return to his room,
I sit on his bed,
I recall his last words,
'I love you Mummy,' he said.

Denise Savage (14)

Close To My Heart

He kicks and screams, and drools and hurts
But he will always be close to my heart
He is always happy to see me when I walk through the front door
He's looking at me with a smile on his face
He likes to try to climb up my arms
He is my baby cousin who is close to my heart.

Nick McCully (13)

Husbands

Husbands, don't they go on?
No matter what you say to them, you're always wrong.
They're always with their mates or down at the bar,
They never stop to think whether or not you'll need the car.

The laziness would make you cry and weep,
They always snore loudly when you're trying to sleep.
Some are sweet and romantic for your benefit,
Most just buy chocolates and flowers for the fun of it.

When it comes to cleaning, husbands are invisible,
Their idea of helping is just plain miserable.
But when it comes to kids, you're safe and sound,
Because an enthusiastic dad is all you'll need around.

Lauren Thompson

My Sister

I love my sister with all my heart,
I always hate it when we're apart.
My sister means so much to me,
But sometimes it is good to be free!

My sister has just turned 18 now,
But we hardly ever row.
My sister will sometimes lend me stuff,
But if it gets dirty, boy she goes in a huff!

I will love my sister forever,
Even though she's not too clever.
I really love making fun of her,
But if I do she just goes grrr!

I really love my sister!

Robyn Conroy (13)

My Pet

My pet is a rabbit,
She walks on all fours,
She lives in the house
But never outdoors.
She eats carrots, bananas
And hates her greens,
She loves to build a nest
And also have a rest.
She is still very young
But very mature,
Her name is Trish
And she is the best.

Richard Barber (13)

My Hero

I admire Tom Delonge from Blink 182
I have respect for him as a person
And as a musician too.
I don't know the words to all their songs
And I don't lust over pictures all day long.
I don't do everything he says
But I'd like to play guitar like him some day.
He has an interest in UFOs
And he sings about them at all their shows.
Tom makes me laugh
He's really funny
He doesn't act like a star
Even though he has lots of money.
I'd love to meet him some day
To tell him he's inspired me in so many ways.
I know I'll be a fan until the day I die
Because Tom Delonge is such a great guy!

Stephanie Murray (14)

Close To My Heart

I am standing here alone and by myself,
I squeeze tightly the small gold locket in my hands
that I will cherish forever,
A cool, chilly breeze that is scented of freshly cut grass blows
against my face,
My long, black hair is tossed to one side and is blowing
in the heavy scented breeze.
I glance up at the cool, clear blue sky,
I can hear birds chirping and humming loudly in the trees filled
with fresh green leaves.
The trees are tall and lean,
Which casts a black harsh shadow on the clean cut grass below,
The trees are packed full of big, pink, beautiful blossoms
which are planted around the wild trees.
My eyes are red and bulging,
A painful tear escapes my eye.
The long, bushy branches are covering you,
I heave the strong, sturdy branch away as the tough branch snaps off
in my delicate hand.
I look to the ground and force a smile,
Pretending you are watching me.
As still as ever stood the black headstone with the italic gold writing
scrawled over it,
There stood your grave all lonely and deserted,
Everyone so busy trapped in their own little world,
Nobody cares . . .
I bury my face in my small hands and cry,
I know you said, 'Do not stand at my grave and weep,'
when you were lying on that damned hospital bed,
But I just want to know the answer to my question,
Why did you leave me?
I am standing here alone and by myself, and I always will be.

Andrea McKeown (14)

Watching Me

I wonder what he looks like,
He'd be eighteen-years-old now.
I wonder what he's doing
Up above the clouds.
I hope he thinks I'm funny,
I hope he thinks I'm kind,
I hope I have the qualities
That he would like to find.
He would be great at football
And popular at school,
He would be kind and listen
And always look really cool.
He died before I was even born,
I hate that I never met him.
I think he would be my best friend,
But I know I'll never forget him.
I love my brother James a lot
And I love Daniel equally,
I hope he knows just how I feel,
But wish that he could see.
Although I wish he was alive
And will always love him deeply,
I feel I have not lost him
As I know he is always watching me.

Lucy Dean (14)

She

There are no words to describe her
A brilliant, sparkling light
She's my one and only survivor
She gets me through the night

And when the times get bad
When I am about to fall
She keeps me thankful not sad
She keeps me standing tall

But now we are moving on
A new life is drawing near
At last my fears are gone
My path is starting to clear

She is my dearest friend
The one I admire the most
A hero till the end
My father, son and Holy Ghost.

Imogen Swart-Wilson (13)

Close To My Heart - A Family Heirloom

A ring - just a ring, golden and rusting,
Passed down to young face from old.
Worn, scratched, in need of a dusting,
Clinging to memories not to be sold.

Memories of babies, red-faced and crying,
Howling, kicking and poorly with flu.
Their mother distraught, tired of lying,
Kids missing the father they never knew.

He left his wife penniless,
Penniless and pleading,
Loans and debts all a mess.
Nobody knew the life they were leading,
Of stealing - being unfair and untrue.
The mother coped from them on, as well as she could,
Five mouths to feed, endless jobs to do.

The ring glints on her finger, winking, reminding
Of the time they were just newly weds.
Young and innocent, happily carefree,
Confetti joyfully thrown over their heads.
It didn't turn out though, as you can see.

He broke the oaths he promised to keep
He was on the run with his wife.
Steely, cold, the knife twisted deep
And that's when she knew he'd ruined her life.

He begged with her, promised he'd change,
But she knew he never would.
Angry and frightened he ran again,
Leaving his family for good.

Sophie Ainscough (12)

I Miss You

Sorry I never came to say goodbye,
Sorry I never saw you one last time.
I wish we could be in the shop laughing and joking,
I wish I could hear you call my name.
Last thing I said to you was see you soon,
I never told you that I loved you,
I wish I did now.
Now you're gone and I know you're in Heaven,
Till that day comes,
I'll be missing you.

Hélène Titus-Glover (14)

Close To My Heart

The things that are close to my heart, things that are dear to me,
Things that everyone in my world can see,
Like rosy-red flowers in the park,
And the shiny bright stars that come out at dark,
The sandy beach and the sun up high,
The great colourful birds up in the sky.

The winter snow on the floor,
The knock of Santa at the door,
The way my family laugh and joke,
The way the fire sizzles when we give it a poke.

My friends and family close to me,
The photos embarrassing as they maybe,
My mum and dad joke and laugh,
My sister runs up the garden path,
My nanna and grandad give me treats,
And give me lots of chocolate sweets.

These are the things that are close to my heart.

Jennifer Fletcher (11)

My World

All fictional books are
False, yet they still leave scars.
They excite and thrill you,
Or leave you guessing who
Commits which crime, which deed -
Whatever, a great read.
You get lost, trapped, captured
In a fantasy world
Where what's actually false
Becomes frighteningly true
To no one else, just you.
Reality, of course -
The people here get on
With their everyday lives.
No adrenaline to thrive
On, back to fantasy . . . gone
Is the temporary world in
Which I live . . . gone is
The excitement I am going to miss.
I'll have to wait
Till the next adventure.

Soraya Collings (15)

Forgotten Bears!

He sits on the shelf
Cold yet loving.
His rough fur, straight ears, small black nose
A familiar, comforting sight.
His miniature paws
Gently holding a tiny pot of jam,
He eats greedily, all the time stationary.
Cold glass, dark wooden doors
Hide his small body.
Shadows fall across his face,
Dust settles on his fur.
He seems sad, forgotten
Just an ornament, untouched, unloved
By the busy surrounding world.
One day he will be brought out into the light,
The dust brushed away,
The doors closed behind him,
So he can take his place once again
Amid the bedcovers and pillows
As a teddy bear.

Lousie Newby (15)

I Admire

The person I admire
Is a person most the world can't forget
What he did mean so much
And some people don't even care

He gave some great speeches
Expressing his deepest feelings
He told the world what he thought
Tried to make it a better place

He never gave up, no matter what
He stuck to what he wanted
He cried out for freedom
Wanted to grab it with both hands.

He wanted equality
No racism and respect
Friendship of two different colours
No matter what anybody said

He succeeded towards the end of his life
His wishes all came true
He should be praised
And we should shout out to
Martin Luther King!

Anjulie Dhillon (13)

Speaking Out

Why do you insist on war?
I thought this was a peaceful land,
And now without a gas mask,
From outside we are banned.

I don't think we're human,
If someone we have known,
Hasn't been hurt or killed;
I feel like I'm all alone.

Our beautiful little country,
Nothing will be the same,
And for what,
A little bit of fame?

Nothing can account for loss,
Of our people who are dead,
Blood flows down the street,
A tear or two is shed.

Something is very wrong,
I feel it in the air,
People are cursing ...
And *bang* ... dead bodies everywhere.

Zippy Jason (13)

You're My Heart's Closest

You're more precious than silver,
More precious than gold,
You're a jewel in my heart, a story untold,
You're my completeness, my song,
You let me know when I'm in the wrong,
You're close to my heart because you're a unique spark.

You're my gift, long-lasting,
Know my problems without asking,
You're kind, sweet and sensitive,
You're my absolute everything,
You're my life's bonus,
You give it extra purpose,
You sometimes give me reason to wanna sing out loud,
With you I can be me and of that I'm proud.

You can always depend on me,
And though we're still young, it's plain to see
That you're close to my heart and I hope we never grow apart.

When I think of you I wonder why God put us together,
It has to be much deeper than my mind can sever,
I look at the stars and think that destiny is what has brought you to me,
I was without you for a while and the length of time seemed
                                        as long as the Nile,

Venus is our planet, knowledge is our shuttle,
One day we'll take off and begin life as a couple.

Fiona McGowan (14)

Companions

A wise man once said
'Great minds think alike',
And I do believe
That he may be right.
Thinking alike
Is a popular trend,
That is commonly found
Between groups of friends.

Friends who stick by you,
Pals who are 'cool',
Buddies who copy
Everything that you do.
Peers who defend you,
Comrades who share,
Best friends that you miss
When they are not there.
They can make you laugh,
They may make you cry,
(You can depend on them
For a good alibi!)
Friends can be young,
Friends may be old,
Friends may be 'weird'
With a heart of gold.

And this is a subject
That is close to my heart -
Those people you miss
When you are apart.

Cayleigh Spooner (16)

Close To My Heart

There is a very special someone
Who is close to my heart,
I'm going to write about them
But I don't know where to start!

They have done so much for me
Over these many years,
When I have fallen down
They have wiped my tears.

I know I should just say it
Or maybe I should hum,
I'm just going to shout it out
I love you Mum!

Alex Hall (14)

Family

What is a family?
Is it a priceless diamond
Mined from the caves of the earth?
Is it a lump of gold
Panned from the longest river?
Is it a smooth white pearl
Plucked from the rarest oyster?
No!
A family is an old cuddly toy -
To be cherished not for its worth,
But for being there,
For being comforting,
For being loving -
Always.

Charlotte Meredith (13)

For The Man

She walks along the platform,
Peering into windows and doors,
Through café entrances and bar shutters
Looking for the man.

The girl pushes her long, thick hair
From her face and clutches
The gift bag
Bought for the man.

She seeks out his majestic shoulders,
His warm palms to place her hands into.
She looks for the weather-beaten hat
Made for the man.

She walks onto the train and through cabins,
Looking up and down the aisles.
She searches,
Searches for the man.

She sees him, her eyes alight
And she rushes down the train flinging
Her arms round his neck, hair and bag forgotten.
'Dad!'

Vicky Clarke (15)

Grandma

Like a lantern shining bright
She let forth a glowing light
Now her light has been put out
She hears no more her children shout
All the games we used to play
To pass us through the summer days
They are no longer daily life
They were cut away with a clean, sharp knife
Though she is not there outside
She teaches me through life to stride.

Kim Hayman (12)

The Photo

As I look up into the photo
In its small rectangular frame,
I see the smiling faces
That I long for in vain.

Whenever there's a problem
I always come to this place,
Here I can always tell them
All my loves and hates.

I love Granny's papery skin,
Grandpa's is still firm.
They never grow thick or thin,
In my memory they still burn.

If I could wish for anything,
I'd wish with all my might,
For Gran and Grandpa to be back
So I could hold them tight.

Hannah Lewis (12)

My Grandad Poppa

I was given two books when Poppa had died,
He had blood-poisoning and had to go to hospital.
His liver wasn't working I heard in horror,
The two old books remind me of him.

He had blood-poisoning and had to go to hospital,
I heard the news after a hot school day.
The two old books remind me of him,
It was the first time someone close in my family had died.

I heard the news after a hot school day,
It was the worst news I've had for years.
It was the first time someone close in my family had died,
I keep the books stored in a safe place.

It was the worst news I've had for years,
I'd be devastated if I lost the books.
I keep the books stored in a safe place,
The books are the things I hold close to my heart.

I'd be devastated if I lost the books,
His liver wasn't working, I heard in horror.
The books are the things I hold close to my heart,
I was given two books when Poppa had died.

Oliver Goulden (12)

My Family

I love them all,
Brothers, sisters, mums and dads.
Mine catch me when I fall,
It's not just a silly fad.

Family are always there,
And always full of care.
Any time you need them,
They will always be there.

Funny dreams, nightmares too,
They will always listen to you.
Whether happy or sad,
They're always glad,
To see you smile,
When things have been bad.

Catherine Fisher (13)

Close To My Heart

He's always there when I need a hug,
He greets me warmly to cheer me up.
He's loyal and sweet,
He's special and fun.
He'll never leave me
Here on my own.
I can trust him with secrets,
He'll never tell.
I love him so much,
He's my dog, Shadow!

Katie Wood (13)

Close To My Heart

My mother said
'Don't do that!'
But I just carried on
She doesn't say it anymore
Because now she's gone.

I miss her smile
And her bright blue eyes
The way she'd hug me tight
I wish she'd come and comfort me
Come and kiss me goodnight.

I think of her differently
Than I used to now
I wish she could have known
How much I loved her
When she was around.

My mother isn't here now
But how I wish she was
I hope she looks down from above
Because now, more than ever
I need her help, guidance and love.

Vicki Bootman (14)

Three Broken Hearts

'Where were you last night?'
Those words echoed inside Brad's head.
Sara had said this trillions of times before he thought.
He could see the sun, sea and sand of where he had last held,
then lost, his girlfriend.

One heart broken

'Do you think I was born yesterday?'
She whispered so no one could hear her rage.
His heart felt like the pounding of the biggest drum in the world.
Flushed, flexile and feisty she walked away forever.

Another heart broken.

'Do I look stupid to you?'
She could have felt his anger a million miles away.
He pushed her out of the door and slammed it with a bang.
Ellie was kneeling, knocking, notifying Jason she was still there.

The final heart broken.

Emma Browes (14)

Deep In My Heart

This thing of mine, the thing I hold
The people in it are my heart and soul
Their friendly faces kind and clear
Scare away both loneliness and fear
As time flies by, this group may fade
But new members will be made
It is amazing where the years have gone
Now new family members are born
I may not know some of my family
Especially the members that have come before me
I have a lot to learn
The trust of some people I have to earn
I haven't been here that long
But still I know right from wrong
All these people are like a sun's ray
And in my heart they will always stay.

Gemma Kellock Ferguson (12)

Close To My Heart

Close to my heart, what do I love?
My friends, my family, the people who care,
When I need them they're always there.
Ring-tailed lemurs with soft grey fur,
Dogs and cats that bark and purr.
The sand, the sea, the warm summer sun,
Chilling out, having fun.
Whizzing down hills on scooter or bike,
Skating and blading are things that I like.
Reading, writing, creating new things,
Being told it's for me when the telephone rings.
Dreaming 'bout acting; films and fame,
Completing a level on a PlayStation game.
Getting a part in the annual school play,
Waking up to a brand new day.
Snuggling in bed on a cold, rainy night,
Friends admitting that I am right.
A bar of chocolate or packet of crisps,
Wood smoke rising in faraway wisps.
Mysteries, legends, fantasy tales,
Bargain clothes in January sales.
Getting letters and parcels just for me,
Eating things I like for tea.
The very first page of a juicy new book,
Hiding away in my own private nook.
Walking around on fresh clean snow,
Being cheered up when I feel low.
Love other people so they can love too,
I'd like to share all my joy with you.

Emily Feltham (13)

Friends And Family

I had a dream last night,
I was flying in the sky,
Meeting old friends and family,
As I passed them by!

I had a dream last night,
I was dancing on the moon,
Dancing happily with strangers,
But hoping to see a friend soon!

I had a dream last night,
I was older, married with kids,
With a nice house and my family,
But without the friends I used to know.

I had a dream last night,
But I can't remember it all,
All I know is I was happy,
With the people I love most!

Sophie Deakin (13)

Close To My Heart

Football is close to my heart
It will always be close to my heart
It has always been close to my heart

Football is my life
It is my career
It's always with me
Close to my heart.

Chris Lishman (12)

The Necklace Tale

This thing is no person
This thing's not brand new
It's a long silver chain
With a small pair of shoes
I've had it for years
And never once thought
How much did it cost
And why was it bought?
It wasn't till recently
I felt really sad
As something had happened
And for me it was bad
I was playing outside
While the sun brightly shone
Then I looked at my necklace
And something had gone!
I took off the necklace
And stared with a glare
As there was now only one shoe
And no longer a pair
I started to worry
And looked all around
And searched through the grass
Which was covering the ground
Although it has changed
And looks out of place
Whenever I wear it
There's a smile on my face!

Katie White (14)

Manchester United

Man United are the best
Better than Arsenal and all the rest
They are even better than Real Madrid
I'm sorry we lost to them the way we did
Beckham is the best player on their team
To play football with him is my dream
Roy Keane is nearly as good
His behaviour, unfortunately, is not as good
Fabien Barthez is quite all right
Except when he plays when there isn't much light
Alex Ferguson is an amazing boss
If he goes there'll be a sense of loss
Old Trafford is so amazing
Some fans just stand there gazing
My ambition is to play there
A Man U shirt I will wear
If I can't play at Old Trafford
I will be a manager there instead
Man United came top of the league
While Arsenal and Newcastle are plagued by fatigue
Man United are the best
Better than Arsenal and all the rest.

Nathan Brown (12)

Close To My Heart

Someone Special

My father he reminds me of a doughnut ...
All soft, round and sweet.

To me he's like a car ...
Simple all the way.

I like to think of him as the Houses of Parliament ...
He's that important to me.

He's like an opera piece ...
Not one for fast pace music.

Like an oak tree, rooted in his business and me ...
Providing me with knowledge I need.

To me he's panda ...
Cuddly and cute.

Just like a diamond ...
Because he's precious to me.

That's my dad ...
One of a kind.

Dearly Important To Me

This person is a cookie to me ...
Sweet, smooth an very important.

She seems to be like Concorde ...
Here, there and everywhere.

She's a five star hotel ...
A warm welcome to anyone.

She is a classical piece of music ...
Calming and relaxing.

She is an oak tree ...
Firm and wise like me.

She says she's a lion ...

Fierce and serious all the time.

She is a pearl to me . . .
Precious and one of a kind.

Who is she I ask?
She is my wonderful *mum!*

Christopher Veazey-Doucet (12)

Vicky

Silent tears stream down my cheeks
As I remember all the good times we had together.
But now they are just a memory,
A distant image blurred in my mind.
My closest friend is gone,
I never dreamt that this could happen.
Not to me, not now.
Somebody, please wake me from this dreadful nightmare.
It can't be true; I must be dreaming.
The sun has burnt out,
The stars have faded,
My whole world is in darkness.
Vicky is dead, she is no longer here.
The smallest things we did together,
I took them for granted then.
They mean so much to me now.
I will never see her beaming smile again,
But she will stay in my heart
Forever.

Alexandra Donaldson (12)

I Can . . .

In Southern Africa lies a jewel,
Although on the map it is an insignificant dot,
It means more to me than if I were given all England to rule.

I can . . .
Remember the stunning sunrise,
The first glimmer of dawn breaking through the darkness,
And you can see the fishermen hauling their catch.

I can . . .
Feel the cool lake breeze on my cheeks,
As the first few fishermen start to come in,
So does the smell of fish - it reeks!

I can . . .
Smell the fear in the air,
It hangs on top of us like a patch of fog,
Leading us further into Mother Nature's lair.

I can . . .
Trust God to guide us,
Through Mount Mulanje's wilderness,
Despite the engulfing darkness.

I can . . .
Picture a whole mountainside,
Covered in a sea of identical green tea bushes,
It's too picture perfect, but I have not lied.

I can . . .
Set my eyes upon Thyolo Mountain,
It is so gorgeous and tranquil,
All it needs is an extravagant fountain, and it'll be ideal.

All these things I will reminisce about,
Malawi, my home is etched in my mind forever,
And I will be back no doubt.

Rosie Ghui (13)

To Fran, My Best Friend

When I cry you cry
You understand

When I laugh you laugh
It's so much fun when we laugh together

You make me laugh, when I cry, in a way that only you can
A joke that's not funny, but you give it that peculiar touch
Our horoscopes say that we will be best friends for life
I didn't need them to tell me, I know we are forever

There is no friendship stronger
You know that it's true
Tested through distance and the slightly insane things that you do
I could not live without you
Even your taste in music I would miss.

Lousie Gamble (16)

Billy

Billy, Billy, what does he do?
He sits down and stares at you.
He chews your tights, socks etc,
And even steals all the letters.

Sleep and play is all he does,
Chewing bones is a habit he has.
He jumps up and down and loves to play,
I hope he calms down one day.

Billy, Billy, what does he do?
He sits down and stares at you.

Fiona Shaw (14)

Siobhan Wood

The one person I admire
Is my friend Siobhan Wood
She never has once let me down,
I don't think she ever could!

Siobhan is very musical,
She plays the clarinet,
She also plays the piano,
She needs to do Grade Two yet!

Siobhan is very quiet,
Well, sometimes anyway,
Especially when she's working hard,
But not when we go to play!

Siobhan's favourite animal
Is of course the dolphin,
I'll think I'll stop this writing now,
Fingers crossed, I'd love to win!

Lisa Goodwin (11)

Still Someone Special

As I sit alone in the coldness of my room,
I listen to the wind strumming my favourite tune.
I can sometimes feel the moonlight gliding over me,
But I never feel his love that was destined for me.
I never hear my phone ring that sweet melody,
When I know he's at the other end waiting to speak to me.
I can't feel all our happiness or even where it used to be,
All his warmth has gone all I know is tears,
And sadly I can't drown them in endless glasses of beer.
I don't know how to end this so I guess I'll just stop here,
Because now I feel the trickling of one lonely tear.

Perri Minton (12)

Mother Nature

She sits there by the flowing river
A fountain of knowledge
A vision of a moonlight night
A diamond in the rough
Her hair the colour of moonlight and sunlight
Entwined in amongst the darkness
Her eyes deep blue merged with sea-green
Sparkling at the wonders of life
Her mind is ever working
Her spirit always aware, alive
The mysteries of the universe
Behold her entranced stare
As she stands and begins to move
With unearthly beauty and grace
She turns to me, I'm noticed
I'm in awe, frozen to the ground
I instantaneously fall under her spell
Her voice is like silk
Smooth yet the echo lingers
She whispers words that are never meant to be heard
And softly glides away
And yet I still cannot move
I'm bedazzled by her aftermath
Mother Nature.

Rebecca Garner (12)

The Fun Is Now Over!

Being little was so much fun,
Giggling and playing in the brightness of the sun.
Life was an adventure,
No worries at all,
But now I have changed
And not for the better.
Showing off, thinking it's clever,
My family and I are growing apart,
I want to be different but where do I start?
I feel so guilty and I know it is wrong,
Now it's been happening for far too long.
My family and friends mean everything to me,
Why can't things be how they used to be?
Inside my raging body my stomach twists,
If I went would I be missed?
School work's going downwards towards the drain,
Attitudes exploding like an atomic bomb inside my brain.
Tears and anger are all I achieve,
A change in me is what I now believe.
Life in the fast lane should come to an end,
It's not really me so why pretend?
A helping hand, a smiling face,
Then my world would be a much better place.
So this is for my mum and dad,
I'm sick and tired of being bad.
It doesn't matter about being 'in with the crowd',
My only wish now is to make you proud.

Amy Burgess (15)

Mum

Mum, you've always been there for me
From my very first steps to my very first words
Without you I am incomplete, without you I am an apple with no core
Mum, you are the best!
With your fine cooking and many varieties of meals,
To vacuuming the floor and washing up,
So I just wrote this poem to show you Mum that I care
And you play a big part in my life.

Christopher Thomas (11)

You

Whenever I'm around you,
I get a funny feeling inside.
Whenever I feel sad,
I look at your smile and I want to smile.
But then I feel sad,
When I don't think of you,
And when I do,
I worry that one day I will lose you.

But if I don't lose you,
Then the world will end,
With only us left.
And only our love will save us.
I know that we will go through a lot together,
But somehow I know that we're meant to be.
I know I will always have a special feeling inside,
Whenever I look at you,
Or whenever we hold hands,
And that feeling tells me that we are meant to be.

Alex Baker (14)

Untitled

There is a rainbow in the sky,
What is it that makes you cry?
Tears running,
Snobs rolling,
Time is going, hurry up,
Cheer up,
There is a rainbow in the sky,
What is it that makes you cry?

Sarah Powell (12)

My Guinea Pig, Scribbles

Munching, crunching,
Chomping through his food,
Running about
Like a little dude.

Charging about
In his run,
Spending all his time
Having fun.

Waking in the morning,
Sleeping in the night,
A cat comes along,
Gives him a fright.

His two front teeth
And his small furry nose,
Gripping on
With claws on his toes.

With a small Mohawk
And a furry body,
He's the number 1 pet
For everybody.

Nicholas Baker (12)

Angel Of Death

The slaves were treated very cruel
Because they were under the pharaohs' rule
The king refused to let them leave
All the slaves could do was grieve
God sent out the ten plagues
Which occurred over so many days

The order came
Put blood up on your door frame
I was getting ready to leave
My family couldn't believe
Thank goodness my child is safe
I think it's because I have faith

My eldest child is dead
I can't sleep or rest my head
I felt like I was whipped with a belt
Freedom at last
Don't mention the past.

Mitchell Lawrence (12)

Love Within

Within my family
Love is so strong
I feel secure
And a huge bond.

Within my family
Trust is there
In my parents
And stays there.

Within my family
Love is so strong
I feel secure
And a huge bond.

Lauren Tovey (12)

Close To My Heart

Most people have a teddy bear,
I am slightly different.
His smell is just as comforting,
My little Indian elephant.

Eyes so understanding,
Of melted chocolate-brown.
They comfort all my sorrows,
In my heart he wins the crown.

Looks at work over my shoulder,
Reads all my books with me.
Someone to snuggle up with,
The first person in the morning to see.

Always there with a kiss and a hug,
Waiting when I come from school.
I don't care what people say,
In my eyes he's really cool.

He'll be there when I'm eighteen,
I'll never give him away.
Let him be threadbare, let him stink,
I love him more than I can say.

Renu Kumar (11)

Close To My Heart

I'm writing a poem
'Close to my heart' is the theme,
I don't know what's close to my heart.
Lots of things are.
I know!
My lungs!
My lungs are close to my heart, in a way,
They are wrapped neatly around it,
I hope I've got the right idea ...

They let me breathe refreshing air,
Though, they also let me breathe repulsive air.
They won't let me breathe underwater,
I found that out for myself!
They inflate like balloons
And deflate like badly punctured footballs.
They're so 'funny' looking,
Yet so useful and functional,
I wonder where I'd be without them ...

I've written this poem now,
'Close to my heart' was the theme,
I know what's close to my heart,
So what's close to yours?

Joseph Steptoe (12)

Guess Who?

He has black hair down to his neck
And eyes that study hard
He likes to eat and have a drink
And is always on his guard.

He's fun to be with that's a fact
And sorts my problems out
A gentle giant he sure is
That seldom screams and shouts.

He knows his way around the globe
Can take us anywhere
He does not need a map in hand
He always treats us fair.

He likes fast cars and football games
And always on the go
I would not swap him for the world
And dearly love him so.

At school he set a record jump
And talks about it still
He played Sunday football weekly
With his mates, Steve and Phil.

He works inside an office block
In charge of many men
He always wears a shirt and tie
Except at home, his den.

They broke the mould when they made him
He's funny and quite mad
A character with love and care
Guess who? He's my dad!

Jak Shinner (12)

Most Dear To Me

(Dedicated to my grampa)

Books and dictionaries cannot see,
To find what a great person you are to me.
I've searched and searched but cannot find,
Your thoughtfulness and why you are so kind.

To find what a great person you are to me,
It's why no other can give as much love as he.
Your thoughtfulness and why you're so kind,
It's why finding you out really blows my mind.

It's why no other can give as much love as he,
How can you be so wonderful? That's what I can't see!
It's why finding you out really blows my mind,
Like a bursting, erupting, cold winter tide.

How can you be so wonderful? That's what I can't see!
And finding you're meaning, my thoughts are so keen.
Like a bursting, erupting, cold winter tide,
My love and thought will never be tried.

And finding your meaning, my thoughts are so keen,
I've searched and searched but cannot find.
My love and thought will never be tried,
Books and dictionaries cannot see.

Sophia John (13)

Close To My Heart

(For Claire Hayes)

I never thought there would be a day, a day when I was lonely
But since you left me here on my own I am feeling moany
You're my best friend and that is true
Being miles apart wouldn't stop me loving you
Once a year I see you now
Why not more, why and how?
So this is for you
You ask me who
My best friend Claire who made me sad
But she is the best friend anyone could ever have.

Katherine Wise (11)

My Family

Family is a special thing
And can never be parted.
That's why I always think about them
Since the day my life started.

Family is like a special parcel,
Always shared around
And the love that shines within it
Fills the earth's ground.

Family means the world to me
And we hate to be apart,
Even though we're sometimes angry,
They'll always be close to my heart.

Catherine & Gemma Salter

Moppet

A cat came to us a stray one day,
Thin and straggly, but wanting to play.
We gave her some milk, which disappeared in an instant,
For two weeks she vanished, my garden I did hunt ...

Finally she came back, this time we gave her some meat,
She stood up on two legs, the cutest thing you've ever seen.
This large, tasty meal, it was a real treat,
She curled up in my arms and had a sweet dream.

Now she'd come every couple of days, ready for some food
and a cuddle,
My dad found her a wooden box where she could sleep,
But when she found she wasn't allowed in the house,
she got in a real muddle.

Later when she was a regular visitor, we let her in all day.
Mum was coming around, so time for the next stage.
It was a cold and wet night, and I was meant to put her out,
but I didn't ...

When Mum found out she wasn't mad, but said, 'You know
she needs a name.'
I thought really hard and came up with not much,
It was then when I started to get my Beatrix Potter books out.

I flicked through the pages and read a few of the stories,
It was back to my childhood but still no names.
I was about to give up when my sister said, 'Look to the back.'
Moppet! Perfect! Now she was really our very own beautiful little cat.

Rachael Tennant (14)

Like I Love You

When I'm down,
Feel like I don't wanna go on,
I don't know what to do,
I turn to you,
I turn to you.

Like I love you,
It's a magical feeling,
It's like a fantasy,
With me and you,
With you and I.

In the good and the bad,
We're together no matter what,
You take care of my heart,
Harm-free and safe,
I love you,
You love me.

You respect me,
Treat me right,
That's why you're my soulmate,
I wanna be with you,
Be with you forever.

Natalie Rogers (12)

My Mum!

I don't really know what to say about my mum,
Except a great thank you to her as I come.
I've known her for the whole of my life,
And have loved her forever preventing strife.

My mum is known right through the town,
As your long-lost grandmother, the caring clown.
She's always there when you need her around,
When you're high in the air, or low on the ground.

Her character appeals to all of my friends,
What way they understand it all depends.
Some find her amusing, loud and long,
Others their angel, someone to look upon.

When exams are near and all hope is down,
She'll put on her dress along with nightgown.
Reassurance she'll give and repeat what she said,
When she was my age and tucked me in bed.

Whatever your problem or achievement may be,
She'll be proud of you, just wait and see.
But one thing I know and can be sure,
Is I'll love her a great deal more than I did before!

Carla Cambridge (14)

Just

You're just a bit of fluff
Just fluff surrounded by mouldy fur
Just two scratched button eyes
Just one brown bead nose

You don't have a heart
You don't have a brain
You can't even console me
Because all you are is fluff

You're just the one who comforted me
And quenched my streaming tears
But you never even spoke a word
Because all you are is fluff

Yet in my head you spoke a thousand words
And the tears that soaked into your matted fur
Made you more a part of me than anyone
You know my deepest secrets
Even though all you are is fluff

And when I have to part with you
When I grow too old
I promise I'll be harder to leave
Than any of those false friends

So before you leave
And enter the dusty attic
I feel you deserve a word
You who have supported me though thick and thin

You old piece of fluff.

Charis Bredin (13)

Guess Who?

Cuddling up close we lie there
As we show the signs of love,
I know he's there cos I can feel him
Twitching like a dove.

The day that I met him
I knew he was the one,
He came up to me and stretched
And his eyes just shone.

His eyes are a greeny colour,
They look at me every day,
His hair is shiny and smooth,
I miss him when I'm away.

My sister chose his brother
At the same time,
Although they had all the attention,
I wouldn't swap hers for mine.

He had all the attention
Because he was the cuter one,
He had the puppy dog face,
It'd be a nightmare if he was gone.

Do you know who he is by now?
The French say, 'Ah le chat.'
Come on think harder … okay,
It's Corkie, my black and white cat.

Danielle Crowson (12)

My Dad

The person I loved most was my dad
When he died it made me sad
His eyes were green
They were the biggest eyes I'd ever seen.

He was a nice natured fellow
Whose favourite colours were red and yellow
He was also very clever
And always complaining about the English weather.

My dad's best friend was my uncle John
They never had any arguments, not one
My dad was perfect in every way
I hope I see him again some day.

Liam Fletcher (12)

My Friends

My friends are always there for me
Whenever I am bad,
My friends will always comfort me
Whenever I am sad.

My friends will never leave me
When I've committed wrong.
Whenever I am feeling weak
They will always keep me strong.

My friends are always by my side
Through times of thick and thin.
My friends will always pray for me
When I'm engaged in sin.

Maria Skoppek (13)

Things That Seem Surely To Be

There are many things close to me,
Things that seem surely to be,
The things that I treasure,
Or even the ones that bring me pleasure.

I'd like to show my appreciation,
To ones who've shown their determination,
In things that seemed so hard,
The way they protect and they guard.

The problems they've resolved,
Or simply the things that I've been told,
The advice they have given,
Or even the things they've forbidden.

All the help over the years,
Brings many tears,
To a man like me,
So the things that seem surely to be.

The things I treasure,
Or even the ones that bring me pleasure,
Is summed up rapidly,
As I love my family.

Carl Ranscombe (14)

Close To My Heart

My little brother,
who I love very much,
is very close to me,
because of this I will hold him
very close to my heart.

My beloved mother,
she does everything for me,
she washes, cooks and cleans.
I love her and she loves me,
she is close to my heart.

My father does the DIY,
he fixes stuff that I break.
I play with these again and again,
remembering that my good old dad
fixed it because of me.
This is why I hold him
very close to my heart.

All of these people I hold close to my heart
because I love them with all my heart.
These people make up my whole world,
they will always be close to my heart.

Henry Matson (14)

My Mum

My mum is the most precious thing to me,
Other people don't understand, they just can't see,
What it means to me to have her around,
Because of the love and peacefulness together we have found.
Most other children don't get along with their mothers;
All they see is useless old bothers,
But when I look at my mum I see a lot more,
I see what my mum is really here for.
She's not there to nag, she's there to keep me straight,
For this other children really do hate,
But I say what's the point in not getting along?
It's like to not have a meaning to write a song.
So I love my mum in every single way,
This feeling gets stronger every single day.
We even go shopping down town together,
Sun, rain or wind, it doesn't matter about the weather.
My mum will drive me places, she really helps me out,
My mum is always happy, she doesn't have to scream or shout.
My mum really is the best,
She's a number one Mum, you can put her to the test.
So when it really comes down to the end,
I'd say my mum is my number one best friend.

Wendy Nesbitt (14)

My Great Gran's Ring

My great gran's ring
Is one of a kind,
Nothing can match it,
So we've never tried.
It's Victorian and fancy
And became mine to own
On the day she died.

My great gran
Was very old.
When she died
We cried and cried.
And all her life
She'd worn this ring -
Apart from when
She lost it.

Then one day
When we stayed overnight,
I saw a dull glint,
And the ring we'd thought lost
Was under the rug
And Gran said when she was gone
I could have it.

So two years ago
When great gran was no more,
The ring became mine
Like she'd promise before.
It's old and it's gold
With a wobbly blood stone.
Rest in peace Gran,
You're always with me.

Charlotte Burton (14)

My Lungs

I can't think of one thing closer
to my heart than these,
they're just below the collarbone
and way above the knees.

They're vital for my living,
they start off pink and clean,
their house is in the rib cage
so from the outside they're not seen.

They're working all the time
and they always try their best,
sometimes they have to work so hard
but they never get a rest.

They're never ever selfish
and they do like to keep clean,
but you make it very difficult
if they're filled with nicotine.

They get a bit confused because
they become black and sticky,
the nose complains it cannot smell,
but they cannot be picky.

The lungs don't understand quite why,
when all they do is good,
they're drowned in all this dreadful stuff
then become hard like wood.

So next time you are tempted
to have a little smoke,
remember your poor little lungs
who *don't* think it's a joke.

Steph Poulson (14)

Unique Friends

My Siamese cat lay on the rug,
I lay down next to her, warm and snug.
Across her body her tail curled,
Oblivious to the rest of the world.

I kiss her head and hug her tight,
Then shut the curtains, shut out the night.
What would I do without you, my beloved friend?
I wish our lives would never ever end.

I could not imagine life without my cat,
Why do I have to think about things like that?
I'll love you forever, I'll keep you in my hold,
Stay with me till the world grows old.

Kelly Hall (11)

The Photograph

Although it may be battered and old
The memory lingers and will never be cold.
A moment captured in the blink of an eye,
Our true colours we don't need to hide.

It can be a special gift to a friend,
Broken bridges it can mend.
Put it in an album or a book,
If you're feeling down just take a look.

Images of laughter, times of glee
Are some of the thoughts it brings back to me.
For a time of remembrance when I am old,
A precious memory to keep and to hold.

The old family you often miss
Are reunited with a kiss.
Hold it forever and don't let go,
Or you'll regret it in a mo'.

Jessica Labhart (14)

A Letter To Grandad

Dear Grandad, how I miss you so,
You left, oh quite some time ago.
No one can sit upon your chair,
No one can fill your presence there.
Your crockery hangs upon the wall,
Waiting for your shadow tall.
The walking stick lies on the bed,
No more paths with you it treads.
And Grandmamma, she misses you,
She just does not know what to do.
But Grandad, don't think of us, in rest,
The victims of your ended quest.
We still love you through those tears of water,
From your loving, dear granddaughter.

Kathryn Conway (13)

Close To My Heart

Close to my heart are my friends,
They're like a circle that never ends.
Where would I be without my friends?
I would probably be looking for new trends.

We have fun my friends and me,
Going shopping and buying CDs.
They're the best people that could be
And close to my heart as you can see.

Friends are great to have around
And comfort you when you're down.
That's why my friends are in my heart,
To help me get over things and make a new start.

Debbie-Marie Watkins (12)

The Pain I Wrote Down In Words

There's hidden shadows all around me,
Reflecting my darkened soul,
Holding more great pain
Than you would ever know.

I can't live without you,
I can't live alone,
I don't want to say the last goodbye,
Don't leave me on my own.

Please don't walk away,
Give me one last chance,
Pull me to my feet,
Take me in your warm, loving arms.

I don't want to lose you,
I can't let you go,
I love you so much
And my love can only grow.

Lauren Thomas (14)

My Idol

My idol? A performer,
Talented beyond my dreams,
Shining so brightly it's blinding -
On mythical, magical screens.

I've committed his face to memory,
Every kink and curl of his hair,
Blue eyes flashing so wildly,
The cameras can't help but stare!

Casey Connor was a bullied boy,
With camera always poised,
Aliens, drugs and football stars -
'The Faculty' is my choice.

His greatest work is an epic,
Its praises I always sing,
Courage flows throughout its length,
It's obviously 'The Lord of the Rings'!

His ebony hair I seek for,
His elfin looks supreme,
Elijah Wood I'll always wish,
To act with on the silver screen.

My idol is an actor,
And acting is my dream,
I want so much to meet him -
On that mythical Hollywood screen.

Kate Barbour (15)

Beanie

Beanie is my very special friend,
I call her Beanie as a name that's pretend!
She's called this because she's so skinny ...
Skinny like a beanpole! Or as a rake,
I'm scared she might break.
She has had strife in her life,
But she'll get through it because she's strong
And knows right from wrong.
When I went on holiday last
I thought and cried for Bean, which sounds daft.
I got a big camel as a pressie for Bean,
When she saw it she thanked me and gleamed.
She's my very special friend is Beanie
And I won't ever forget her because that just wouldn't be me!

Jackie Heath (15)

About My Mum

When I was small
And started to cry
Who was there
To wipe the tear from my eye?

If I had a cough or cold
Who was there for me to hold?

She's always there after school
She's always acting very cool!

She will still be there when I'm grown up?
And I bet she still calls me a mucky pup!

Emma Murphy (11)

Sir

Everyone cheers his name,
Everyone loves his game,
He has an expensive taste,
But what he buys does not go to waste.

He wants people to know who's boss,
If they don't listen, then they get lost.
His passion for the game is great,
But what he does hate is to wait.

He cheers us up when we are down,
He has been knighted, although he should have been given the crown.
People say he is not the best,
He doesn't even compare to the rest.

No one dares answer back,
For they will get more than a slap.
His desire for the game
Is always in admiration, not in vain.

Have you guessed who this poem is about?
You should have done by now,
If not don't shout!
It's Sir Alex Ferguson.

Tom Jewell (14)

First Memory!

I was about five-years-old
Waiting for the ride,
I was standing by the door
On the right-hand side.
Dad crawled in
On his hands and knees,
'Fancy a ride?' he asked.
'Yes please!'
I jumped on his back,
My sister stood behind,
'Forward!' I called,
Having fun was on my mind.
We went through the hall
And to the study door,
Dad stopped for a second
Then dropped me on the floor.
I started laughing
As I got up off the floor,
I started shouting,
'More, more, more!'
This is my first memory,
It's very close to my heart,
It's really special,
From my heart
This memory will not part.

Stephanie Morrison (12)

My Pet Dog

I really love my pet dog Charlie
And he loves the taste of barley.
He likes to eat all kinds of stuff,
Eating bricks and acting tough.
I love him more than words can say,
Please don't take my dog away.
With soft, short fur and a very long tail,
So clever is he to bring me the mail.
The long enjoyable walks in the summer,
I wouldn't swap him for any other.
He's more of a brother, than of a pet,
The noise he makes I just cannot forget.
Tug of war is his favourite game,
But sometimes he can be a real pain.
His innocent look, his beady eyes,
Don't stop him from eating juicy flies.
Me and my dog are close to heart,
That's why we don't ever part.
Charlie is very special to me,
Wherever we are, on land or sea.
He always has been good to me,
Always has and forever will be!

Aimeé Baxter (13)

The End

What is the reason for me staying here?
Each time it's so painful crying a tear.
It's times like this I feel death's a new life,
And how unreal it is to become someone's wife.

Why is each day so cruel and unkind,
The bad things in life God just doesn't seem to mind.
Next time I decide to start something new,
I'll be reminded of now and won't know what to do.

When I sit here and think as I read through my book,
And remember those things I had that he took.
I'll remember those promises he made to me,
I forgave and forgot and just left them to be.

Now I realise that I should have been stronger,
How the hell can I make this last much longer?
It's a secret that I will hide inside,
But where is my dignity where is my pride?

I just build it all up and try to pretend,
But it's life and I know it will come to an end.

Amie Swainland (17)

Celadon

*(This poem is a memory of mine about my mum, brother and me
in a field playing when I was young, and again when I was older)*

Orchard winds awoke you from your laze,
I a little boy, running through the long, sweet lyme grass,
To you; the dusk garden blossomed by white light.
Flying right behind you we roll through,
Tamed grass and killed flowers.
Swinging round in circles,
Falling to the ground with rings of roses.
Fair of face is Monday's child that you hug,
With tender apple soothed chest nurtured by hands,
Crafted by watered down arguments and blackberry pickings I'm;
Cradled across tractor fought weeds,
Your strawberry bleached cheeks and cherry-blue lips, sugared.

At present clambering against festering heat-fed reeds,
Sweltering in the timber rotted water,
I remember of,
Being sung stories to me at twilight,
Kissing me that goodnight away with coffee-stained, lipstick breath,
Comforting when dark thoughts crept across the floor.
Now, sitting near the flax-dam punished by heat,
Worn, withered hands bathe in murky silt,
Frumpy floral patterns cover your figure,
Enriched by the smell of baking and whitewashed perfume,
A frail smile and then;
Staring into your lost celadon eyes,
I realise,
The long day is over.

Andrew James (15)

Great Grandma

Sadly on the 2nd May, the year 2003,
My great grandma passed away at the age of 93.
One more month, she had to go, to become aged 94,
Which for many of us to think of is an achievement, I am sure.
Eight years ago she fell ill and had to go into care,
So to Fairhavens she went and was very happy there.
She made new friends, met old ones and kept the ones she had,
All of which I think, are feeling very sad.
I loved my great grandma from the bottom of my heart,
But I know now in Heaven, she will be making a brand new start.

Victoria Handley-Garland (12)

Untitled

Tried to write a sonnet
But they redefine 'hard'
And I could not do it.
I could have bought a card
To tell you how I feel
But they were clichéd and
Foul. I needed something real
And from heart to hand
To you. It's tough to say
How I care just for you,
And I never found a way
To prove my love is true.
So I'm back at the start
With you breaking my heart.

Hannah Pearson (14)

Close To My Heart

Our eyes glancing across the classroom
Every time I see you I blush.
You smile at me, and I smile back
Will you be my first or last crush?

You ask me to meet you after school
There I stand waiting for you,
In the cold, icy streets
Shall I stay, or look for someone new?

I've always liked you,
But you just don't know it.
Will my dreams ever come true?

As I peer down each street,
I see nothing but darkness,
Will you be there? Will we ever meet?

All I want is to hold your hand
As tears fill my eyes,
I shiver with cold,
All the things you said to me, were they all lies?

No, there you are smiling at me,
You're looking really cool but smart.
I'm glad you're there for me,
You are very close to my heart.

Claire Battersbee (14)

Friends

Baby don't cry
No matter what
Our love won't die
Not as quick as that

You were given to me
Given to me as a gift
A gift that will always be
A gift that I will always lift

Through hours, days and years
Our love surpasses all
It revolves around us like spheres
Spheres that always recall

You were there
You will always be
You are here
Right next to me

Always, a love from a friend
Who always cares
About you to the end
A friend you can declare

Something about you
Makes me stay
Close, because you love me too
And to that I give praises every day.

Ennie Ulaya (15)

The Friendship Race

You have to stretch just before a race
With all intentions of getting first place

Pick your race by type and speed
Leave out the ones that you don't need

Be sure to know your limitations
Bad choices can lead you to incarceration

Before you start you must measure your bar
If this is forgotten you will not go far

Keep your focus, don't lose concentration
You won't win if you fall into temptation

You're almost ready, just keep track of time
Good friends are too hard to find

Now we're running, we're going fast
We're almost sure our friendship will last

Have a technique that you can follow through
So you'll have a best friend to run to

Don't go too fast, don't go too slow
Keeping your pace will help the friendship grow

Finally it's over, the race is done
We didn't get first place, but our friendship, *we won!*

Danielle Carr (13)

Hate!

I thought there was a Cupid,
But now there's little miss hate,
How long will she keep my heart black?
I'll have to see, I'll have to wait.

Hate swarms you with disturbing dreams,
Crashing down on you those screeching screams.
Like sitting carefully on a stone wall,
Until you start crying beginning to fall.

Hate has hidden the flowers and love,
And has a crow taken the goodness from a dove?
The world is mixed with different emotions,
Hate has scattered them across all oceans.

Filling me with fury,
Don't you know?
No, probably not this time
I *hate* you though!

Megan Styles (12)

My Friends

I'll start with the loud one
Lauren is her name
She's really quite insane
She never stops giggling
And her tummy is wiggling
She loves to be singing
We can't wait for the bell to be ringing.

Next comes Chloe
A little quieter this time
Not much mind
She goes to dancing classes
Where all her time passes
She cheerleads for all the footie teams
And on her face is a huge beam.

Last but not least is Rachel
You'd think she's the quiet kind of girl
With her fringe in a curl
Rachel really is quite loud
You'd never think it out aloud
Trampolining is her hobby
Up in the air and so floppy.

We may all be different
But we're all ...
Best friends!

Abigail Herring (12)

Nostalgia

I use to go to her house
And the nostalgia hit me
I hadn't known her long
So she wasn't the memory
In that house was a trigger
And I'd remember a beach
I'd remember the heat
I'd remember the cliffs
I'd remember the sea
I'd remember a shop full of dolls
There would be music and flashing lights
At night and then the holiday would begin again
The next day we'd back at the beach ...
I remember lazy days.

Clare Stone (16)

I Remember

I remember the time my parents told me I was leaving my school ...
The way my friends looked as I told them.
The sideways glances as I went past,
The silence that came upon the class,
The looks on their faces.

I remember the huddled, whispering groups in the corner ...
The way they'd all want to sit next to me.
The notes that went flying around the room.
The way the air seemed filled with gloom.
The whispers, the smiles, the tears, the laughter -
The day I left.

They were so happy!

Rhianna Moss (13)

Close To My Heart

Dad

Every time I get sad or down,
I call upon my favourite man,
He cheers me up
And makes me laugh,
My favourite lad, I love you Dad.

Mum

Mum, you solve my problems,
Mum, you help me with worries,
Mum, you are so special,
Mum, you make me feel safe,
Mum, you light my path,
Mum, I love you.

Claire Woolcott (12)

My Friend Judith

M   is for her musical talents,
Y   is for her youthful smile.

F   is for her friendly attitude,
R   is for her respect for others,
I   is for her interesting hobbies,
E   is for her energy,
N   is for her neat hair,
D   is for her dazzling dress sense.

J   is for her jolly laugh,
U   is for her will to understand,
D   is for the way she's so docile,
I   is for her ice-cold hands,
T   is for her taste in food,
H   is for being herself.

Joy Dorman (13)

The Beach

Shimmering water gleaming greeny-blue,
The wave crashing helping the surfers move,
A high-pitched sound occurs, the dolphins are singing,
The golden sand slowly moves in the chilling breeze,
Palm trees drop coconuts to the ground,
Which break to release a watery solution.

The sun is setting over the sea - reds, oranges and yellows,
Just enough light to collect seashells,
And walk along the ocean front.
The waves cover my feet again and again,
It feels cool but soothing.

It's getting cooler as the night sky darkens,
The tide's coming closer to me,
I'd better get home.
I climb the cool, stone steps to a street,
I take one look back and think to myself,
I'll be back tomorrow!
And slowly walk away.

Emma Plowright (12)

Close To My Heart

I have many things that are close to my heart,
I think of them when I am alone in the dark.
My mum, my sister, or my dad,
All the thoughts are far from bad.
My horse, my dog, or my cat,
I think of them in the place where I'm sat.
I love them all so, so much,
I could not live without their touch.
They help me through real bad times,
At whatever hour the big clock chimes.
When I am feeling down and out,
They stop me from feeling the need to shout.
When I am feeling on top of the world,
All my thoughts are twisted and twirled.
It's more than a feeling being with them,
It's more than a feeling since I was ten.
I can see clearly when they are around,
Even if not one of them makes a single sound.
When I am around them I am like an albatross,
When they are gone I'm like a small piece of moss.
If my family and loved ones were not here,
My life would be simple, and played by ear.
'Take your life on the run,' they say,
'I am sure it will be better that way.'
When I am with them I have a great time,
They will stay close to my heart for all time.

Luke Maynard (15)

Lottie

You dart about like a maniac
You twist and swerve and sway
But yet I could not give you back
To that place you used to stay.

You drive me mad
But you're not all bad
You sometimes act quite sweet
You're not what I'd call clever
But you'd do anything for a treat.

Your breath might stink
And your teeth might sink
Into my favourite toy
But I wouldn't swap you any day
You bring me too much joy.

Eleanor Skuse (13)

Busted

Busted are my favourite band,
Concert tickets are in demand.

James is fit and really cool,
He is sometimes silly and acts the fool.

Mattie is funny and pulls strange faces,
With the band he travels places.

And finally Charlie last but not least,
He has his hair in spikes
And rides BMX bikes.

I think this band is really fab
Every time I see them I always go mad.

Gemma Astbury (13)

Why?

Why
Have you taken my family and friends away?
You have left me with no happiness at all.
I have been gliding around all day searching for food.

I have not had a proper meal for weeks.
Where have all the shoals of fish gone?
You have wiped out my food supply.
My eyesight is starting to fail me and I cannot breathe properly.

If I come up to the slippery, slimy surface
I know that you will be waiting for me.
Surely there are better things to do on Earth, than capturing and killing dolphins?
My fins are a lost child's rubber shoe.

I am a mammal just like you.
Why do you want to harm such intelligent animals like me?
I have only ever helped you.

You all have families like me.
You must hate it when you get split up from each other.
And you want them back.
Well that is exactly how I feel.

I have been waiting for you to come and catch me.
I know you are going to get me eventually.
What gives you the right to destroy my life,
My family and my friends.

I am lonely like an orphan waiting for someone to rescue him.
There is no one else left, I am the last of a kind.
What is the point in trying to survive,
If you are going to kill me anyway?

While you have choices, I have none.
I can hear the sound of rumbling thunder.
I cautiously peep out of the water to see what it is.
My head explodes and there is blood all around.

Kim Grewal (12)

Desperate Love To Say

Life is going like a heavenly dream,
Filling my heart with love to its brim.
Words my love, I would like to say,
A million times as you come up my way.
I will bring the sun to make you smile,
Just to admire, throughout the life of time.
If the moon and the stars make you glad,
My love for you drives me mad.
All your worries will fade in vain,
For under my care not a feather, be a pain.
Like a jewel in the crown, your beauty
Shines like a star in the rarest galaxy.
Your verdict really means my world,
With passion, to the gods I lift my sword.
These are secrets confined within me,
As no one will sing this saga for me.
It is a fear that prevents me to tell,
But patiently waits for you to ring a bell.
Love is paper, life is glue - I want to say,
You are my heart, thus need no clue.
I love you girl. Do you?

Mutukkumar Dhashinamoorthy (16)

Foxy

When people look at Foxy, some think he's a dog!
Me - I know he's a fox.
His large beady eyes shine with goodwill
Towards his fellow friends on the window sill.
He has an earnest expression of foxiness,
A stout stubborn nose
And fat little feet that could never be mistaken for your everyday toes.
Foxy has an organic air -
With his summer suit and flowery cap propped
Up on his short stubby hair,
Where I once cut because I thought it would grow back
And one of his legs is bandaged tight,
After an incident in a fight.
Foxy is remarkably unique,
The way you nod his head to make him squeak.
The way he could never tumble when you flicked him on.
He can just move his mouth and attempt to yawn,
When I saw Foxy lying dumped on the stage,
In my old primary school autumn sale.
He sent out a signal that seemed to say -
Please come over and take me away,
And so I handed over one single 5p
And from then on -
I guess -
It's been Foxy and me.

Latifa Akay (14)

Butterflies

I love the way you look at me
That funny feeling inside of me
The butterflies come and I start to blush
And I lose myself in the adrenaline rush

I love it how you make me feel
When your eyes meet mine and nothing feels real
And all that really matters is what's here right now
Then suddenly it's gone and time's passed us somehow

So before any more hours slip to days
I've just got something I'd like to say
The first time I saw you, the first time we met
I knew it was love and our path was set

I don't want to spend another moment wondering
If we could have been, if I had said something
So with one deep breath, I'd like to say,
'Will you go out with me, some day?'

Georgina Le Flufy (14)

He

He is the one whom I like
He is the one who starts all the fights,
He is the one whom I love,
He is the one who coos like a dove.
He is to me a precious pearl,
He is the one who says, 'I am but a girl.'

He is the one who treats me like dirt,
He is the one the other girls will flirt.
He is the one who disrupts my mind,
He is never to me, just and kind.
Yet he is the one whom I still like,
He is the one whom I still love.

Gemma Arnold (13)

Mothers . . .

Mothers are angels sent from the kingdom of love,
Mothers are red roses, so delicate, so beautiful.
Mothers are the smell of strong fragrances,
sweet senses we can always recognise.
Mothers are golden sunshine, bright, warm and blissful.
Mothers are musical boxes, singing sweetly
to that lullaby which sends me to the Land of Nod.
Mothers are hearts of solid gold, a heart filled
with an everlasting love.

Lauren Davies (13)

They're Special

My dad he works day and night,
Just to make sure we're living all right.
My mum looks after my baby sister
And when she's gone, we really miss her.
My sister she goes and works at school,
And her big sister is really cool.
My baby sister has a lot to say,
But we love her in every way.
My dad, my mum and my two sisters are the best family,
And I just think I'm very lucky to have them here with me!

Holly Barbara Montague (11)

A Special Memory

I was trembling as I mounted the long flight
of steps to the top.
My legs were like jelly - shaking and white,
I longed to stop.

But something kept me going - drove me on
and despite my fear,
I kept going strong.

I was nearly there,
my fear growing stronger,
washing over me like
a huge wave of fright.

I'd reached the top - boarded the platform
which would determine my doom forever ...

My legs were poised on the edge,
my arms were above me in an arc,
I'd looked down at the water below -
shimmering, slightly sinister and dark.

Who knew what terrors that rippling surface hid?

I took a deep breath,
and leapt off the board
it surely meant death,
as through the air I soared.

But suddenly all my fear was gone - I was flying like a bird,
my body poised in a beautiful arc ...
I hit the water and dived beneath.

Down ... down ... down!

I'd resurfaced gasping and in that moment, realised I'd done it!
I'd fulfilled my dream and beaten all the fear I ever had.

What a special memory to keep stored up
in a special place in my heart!

Melek Akay (12)

When They Were Going

I stretched and sprawled,
With my legs curved artistically towards the skyline.
I moved towards a terrifying surprise
Which waited for me,
Like an animal pouncing with strong paws
On its prey.

I searched again, yet in vain,
To find myself in an envelope of despair.
Waiting, hoping and finally turning.
Twisting to the other side to see
A wrinkled, worried lady
With deep loving eyes, looking through to me.

I too looked
But found no definite answer to my simple question.
They should have told,
They should have whispered, whined, yelled.
Anything!
So I would be the first to know, instead of the old lady.

Indusha Selvanathar (13)

Forgive Me

Oh thoughtless word and wordless thought,
Which spring into my lips unsought,
Which in my heart account to nought,
Oh thoughtless word and wordless thought.

Cosmo Grant (11)

True Love

True love never runs smoothly
And the most beautiful of creatures
Doesn't have a face
The sweetest thing looks bitter
And paradise doesn't seem like a place

My heart is always happy
But at the same time my heart weeps
Because it's always sad
And when I cry, I smile
And tears come when I laugh

And when I think of you and I'm happy
And when I don't and I start to feel sad,
But the tears won't come
And when nothing seems to go right
Then we'll know that it's true love

When this love doesn't run smoothly
And our beautiful angel of hope
Doesn't have a face
And they think our sweet love seems bitter
And don't think our paradise is a place

True love never runs smoothly
So if we make it through all life's obstacles
Our love will last
And you'll be in my heart forever
As long as the years shall pass.

Victoria Bates (14)

That Special Something

A part of me is missing
When they are not there,
That space in me is filled
Greater as they care.

My love for them as they for me
Is like the blazing sun,
Alive for eternity
Is how it should be done.

A flood of hope runs through my veins
As they approach me close,
Their gleaming eyes and loving faces
As gentle as a rose.

They shower my world with precious gifts,
I'd be lost without them around.
The gifts of love, care and happiness,
You need love, the most I've found.

There's just one more thing I can truly say
As happy as we may be
We sometimes have some arguments,
But I still love my family.

Natasha Edwards (12)

My Loveable Puss

My best pet Tibby,
The tabby and white cat.
She miaows every day of the year,
Her purring sounds like tumbling rocks.
She licks herself clean, perfectly soft,
She licks me morning and night.
Munch, munch, munch, she goes with her food,
My best pet Tibby.
Jumping and leaping over fences and hedges,
Hiding amongst the bushes.
Sheltering from the rain,
When hot, she does the same.
She sits by the fire,
Snoozes and snores for hours on end,
She's warm and loving,
My best pet Tibby,
She whips her tail from left to right,
I love my best pet Tibbs.

Alex Capewell (11)

Teams

There are lots of teams
Football, rugby and other teams
I'm in teams. Are you in teams?
Some teams win and others lose,
Teams make you a lot of friends
Teamwork is the key to glory.
I love teams!

Luke Page (12)

Close To My Heart

As I thought of a person close to my heart
I was thinking of someone I couldn't bear to part
Who was there to see me laugh and play?
Who did I want to see at the end of each day?

At first I didn't know what to do,
All these thoughts - him, her or you!
But this person, you will see
Will always be in my memory.

He may have died when I was small
When I hardly knew about him at all
But I remember how he played with me
And taught me my numbers and ABC.

And though he'd grow tired and have a quick sleep
Right by his bedside I wanted to keep
Then when he went, people said, 'Make a fresh start.'
But my grandad he, will always be, close to my heart.

Laura J Howarth (13)

Double Trouble!

My sister and I have a lot of fun
We make a lot of noise, especially on the drum.
We wriggle about when we go to sleep
And in the car, we press the horn, *peep!*
Although we do have many fights,
We cheer up and play under the blankets
And when we do, she bites.
But we still have our love for each other
Anyway, here comes Mum, Dad and brother.

Manveer Batebajwe (12)

Emotion

I remember when it happened
I was only five,
The memories I have are all
blurred and disguised.
Losing someone close to your heart
is just like your world falling apart.
No one can help, no matter what they do,
the only person you can depend on, is you.
Trying hard to get on with my life,
The pain still hurts like a knife!
I try not to cry, I try to be strong,
but I still can't believe that you have gone.

I can't hear your voice, I can't see your face.
Why, oh why, did this have to take place?
Questions running through my mind,
but I can't answer them now, maybe another time.
I try to be something I'm not, but I'm still here
because you're all that I've got.
If I stumble and fall, should I get up and carry on?
I wish you were here to see me shine!
I want to be like you, loving and kind.
                                My mum!

Nicole Kelly (14)

Parents

Parents can be tight sometimes,
But you should never fight.
They make you wear just one inch heels,
Say, 'Switch off that bedroom light!'

But we should always love them,
No matter what they say or do.
Because they only want what's best for you,
So can you really do without that, too high shoe?

So lighten up, do what they say
And you will really fly!
So stop just doing what *you* think,
And just try!

So girls ditch those silly shoes,
And boys stop asking for new footie boots!
So stay in school, don't be a fool.
Have a laugh! It'll be a real hoot!

Before I go, I'd like to say,
Treasure your parents or they'll go away.
With patience and with love,
When you grow old, you'll have a lot to say.

Laura Greenfield (11)

Memories

Memories, everyone has childhood memories,
Even if they are sad memories.
Some could be happy,
Some could be hilarious,
You need some way to remember the dog who died
When you were only little.
The dog who loved water,
The dog who played with you
When you were sad.
The dog which your dad buried in the garden
Of your old house.
When you couldn't stop crying -
That memory is mine!
Everyone should try and remember the good times,
They are so much better than the sad ones.
Memories!
Memories of Milly.
You could have memories of the Iraq war,
Because maybe, you were there.
I feel very sorry for the families who lost their beloved
Son, husband, uncle, dad, brother or even their daughter.
Memories!
Think of the good memories of those families who lost
Someone special to them in their family -
Like it is for me with my dog Milly.

Edwina Blake (15)

Close To My Heart

Celebrities, celebrities; all that fame,
Being a celeb is one big game,
Pop stars, actors and all the rest,
It's all about being the very best.

New celebs come and go,
But how to be one; I don't know.
All the fashion and the money,
They're so rich, it's kind of funny.

I'd love to try out their lifestyle,
But only for a little while.
A celeb; I'd love to be,
But I know it won't happen to me.

Abby Lee (12)

My Brother Adam

My brother Adam is as thin as a stick
At answering questions he's incredibly quick.
He loves to mess and joke around,
And shake his body to some groovy sound!
You should see his room, it's like a pigsty,
I'm sure under that rubbish, there's an old apple pie!
He loves footie matches, he goes with my dad,
If he ever missed one, he'd be mad and sad.
He's good at it too, football I mean,
Adam's the best 12-year-old player,
I've ever seen!
I'm 13 years old, making me his big sis,
If he ever misses facts, this is *one* he does miss!
When we're older, I want to keep in touch,
Because you see I love him very, very much.

Francesca Henry (13)

Someone I Admire

There is someone whom I admire
Whose career is my true desire
Someone who is a well-known and a famous singer
On whose lyrics in my thoughts do linger
Someone who tells it like it is
Whose music to listen to, is pure bliss
Someone whose lyrics I can relate to
Whose music is different and new
Someone who knows their own mind
Who never leaves their dreams behind
Someone is proud to be who they are
Will always shine like a star
Someone who knows exactly who they want to be
Whose songs mean so very much to me
Someone whose songs I could never hate
Who is talented and great
Someone whose albums I could listen to all night
I would love to write songs like they write
Someone who is the best -
Who is a million times better than all the rest
Someone whom I will never forget
She is the one and only Alanis Morissette.

Rebecca Jade Groves (14)

Close To My Heart

The day is bright,
The day is dull,
No matter what
You're always close to my heart.

You're like a shield for protection,
And knows what's right for all.
You're big and brave and you face the truth,
Just like a leader, leading all.

Whenever I'm faced with a problem, you give me hope,
Whenever life's hard, you help me cope.
Whenever I'm down, you make me laugh
Whenever I'm bored, you make life fun.

The day is ending
I have so many thoughts,
Then I think of you
And there's peace at last.

You're always there for me, when I need you most,
When you're around, there's no need to feel low.
You're kind and considerate and never tire,
So I just like to say *thank you* again.

When I'm hurt you comfort me,
Whenever I cry, you stop my tears,
When there's a fight, you sort it out,
When you need a friend, you know where to come.

You help those in need,
Make them feel wanted,
We keep ourselves close,
As if we are sisters.

So many good times we've had
So many yet to come -
So let's make this friendship last
Forever and ever.
Cos I'm not sure what I would do if you were ever to go.

Saera Sulthana (12)

Close To My Heart

Flooding the world
With learning and light,
When He died for me
He never put up a fight.

Giving Himself up
To pain and sadness,
So we could be saved,
In joy and gladness.

The best part to
This so-called end of the tale,
Was that even when deserted,
He would never ever fail!

Then He rose again,
Though in death's grip of ice,
My Saviour, my friend,
My Lord Jesus Christ.

Charlie Goodwin (12)

A Time To Remember

There's a time I remember from a long time ago
with rainbows, sunbeams and crisp white snow.

This special time is quiet and shy,
it burns like fire in a bottle I hide.

It's a secret time, close to me in a faraway place, where I can be free.

It's a time I will treasure till the end of my days,
it's a time I spent with my family on holiday.

Ruth Singleton (15)

My Kitten

The little wet nose,
The small brown paws,
The tiny blue eyes
But that was before.

Now she's an angel,
My baby so sweet,
Her name was Button,
Our love could not compete.

I can't believe she died at all,
I've never cried so hard,
I love her still; she's in my heart,
She'll never flee a yard.

She was a baby Siamese,
She did look kind of funny,
Her ears were big, yet she was small,
She cost us so much money.

She cost us that, but in my heart,
She was always priceless,
She isn't dead, she's alive
Her soul cannot be lifeless.

She filled that gap that was inside,
I told her why I was sad.
I know that one thing's for sure -
She's the best Siamese I ever had.

Rebecca Goodrum (12)

Friends

Friends are always there for you,
When you're happy or feeling blue.
Go to them to have a chat,
They're all different, thin or fat.
You can tell your friends anything.

Monday morning when you get to school,
You're happy to see them, they are so cool.
Your first lesson may be maths,
You enjoy it because of the laughs.
School is boring without them.

One day when you're in the yard,
Something hits you really hard.
It's not the football,
It's them, leaving you against the wall,
It's never great when they leave you out.

You go to talk -
They go for a walk.
You think about all the laughs,
Why does next lesson have to be maths?
It's not right, sitting alone.

After a day or two
You're still feeling really blue.
They come over to you -
They start to talk and they say sorry too.
Falling out isn't very nice.

Friends are always there for you,
When you're happy or feeling blue.
Go to them to have a chat,
They're all different, thin or fat.
You can tell your friends anything.

Sarah Boardman (13)

My Gran

My gran was very important to me,
As she preserved all the family memories.

My gran was always kind and caring,
She loved to see us kids being nice and sharing.

My gran was a very generous person,
She never stopped us from doing things we wanted to try.

My gran had respect for everyone,
She never insulted anyone.

My gran taught people to believe in themselves,
Now I can achieve anything myself.

My gran always gave help to all the family,
I've now learnt to appreciate people for what they are.

My gran supported me in everything I did,
She made me feel I was always wanted.

My gran would always encourage me,
That's why I want to preserve all the family memories.

Vicki Bennett (15)

She

She is my taxi
She is my cook,
She is my dishwasher
She is my washing machine,
She is my bank
She is my cleaner.

She is my teacher,
She is my shelter,
She is my fairy godmother,
She is my watcher,
She is my light,
She is my friend.

She is my mum.

Michelle Haythornthwaite (15)

Frozen Photo

A smiling face,
A frozen face,
Her eyes do not twinkle.
Still as a statue,
Straight as a pole,
Her body stands forever.
She was just a photo,
A peaceful photo,
In which her body could be seen,
But her soul - not.
I wish the photo would open and give her back to me,
I held the photo close to my heart,
Wishing that she was here for me,
But no . . .
It was just a photo.
A frozen photo,
A selfish photo.

Anjani Vedula (12)

The Lake

Surrounded on all sides by mountains
Tall and jagged they stood, their craggy faces
Portraying not the slightest hint of mercy.
Earth's eternal guards, timeless
And there is was, the lake!
Seemingly untouched by man's destruction
Like Heaven on Earth
Salvation for the good.
The surface was calm and tranquil
Its blue depths never to be seen
It spreads out into a wide oval
Its edges, lapping at the shore.
The smooth stones, ground by the waters of time
Sparkled and glimmered in the sun,
The sandy earth creating a home for each stone
However small.
Thick grass covers the hillocks like a carpet,
Nature's carpet, all is still
And now you wish to sleep here for eternity
And watch the uncharted worlds of stars by the lake.

Krish Chedumbarum (14)

Brothers And Sisters

Brothers and sisters are two of a kind,
Sometimes they're funny and sometimes they're mad.
They use your things and wear your clothes
Sleep in your room when you're not there,
Break your CDs and ruin your room.

What will I do, they're everywhere?

Carly Bamford (13)

Gone!

Myself, my mum and my two brothers
Moved to Cornwall and left the others.
The rest of the family were sad to see us go
And even I was feeling low.
I hoped I'd see them all again soon
But they only come and visit once in a blue moon.
350 odd miles or so is a long way to travel, I know
Although being a long distance apart,
I love and miss them, deep down in my heart.
Maybe when I'm old enough to live on my own
I'll move back to Birmingham and get my own home.
That way I'll be happy and the rest of the family too,
But I don't think that will happen, do you?

Heidi Kennedy (13)

Football

Football is the best,
Better than all the rest,
Football is real cool,
My friends and I play it at school.

Sometimes we lose,
Sometimes we ... win!
Sometimes we just play for fun,
But we're still better than everyone!

Sometimes we don't play at all,
Usually we fall ...
But hey, who cares because we're
Simply the best - better than all the rest!

Margaret-Rose Murphy (12)

My Granny

A big part of my heart
belongs to my granny.
It's like a wonderful art,
as her face is printed all over it.
Sometimes I can be a pain to her
but she would never murmur.
That's why a big part of my heart belongs to my granny.

My granny is close to my heart,
although she calls me a *fart!*
She has 14 grandchildren,
(with another on the way!)
But it wouldn't make any difference
Oh God, no way!
That's why my granny is so close to me
and I just thought I would say.

Chris Newell (13)

What Is She?

I have a pet,
She is invisible.
No one can see her but me.
What is she?

I have a pet,
She can go through walls,
I want to too.
What is she?

I have a pet,
She scares me sometimes,
When she goes -
Boo!

Kathryn Isaac (13)

In Loving Memory Of Tupac Shakur

I quickly switch on the television and hear the loud, echoing shots
being fired.
As I saw two brass bullets soaring violently towards his
unexpecting chest.
Then a loud, eerie scream was expelled from his widened mouth.
The disgusting bright red blood flowing freely from his open wound,
as frightened onlookers stare in total and utter amazement.
Nee! Nooa! Nee! Nooa! The blue flashing lights alarm us
that the ambulance is here and reminds us that we're not dreaming.
The ambulance door slams shut with a bang as two strong men
jump out carrying their extremely large first-aid kits and a bright
protruding orange stretcher.
They ran to the smashed-up black BMW with the bullet holes
advertised on the right hand side, as they clamber inside to the
injured victim. They discuss his state and transfer his injured body into
the waiting ambulance, which was stationary for five minutes,
then they sped away like a bat out of Hell!
His body was lying there in the uncomfortable, lumpy ambulance bed,
cold as ice and hard as stone.
The hospital pronounced Tupac Shakur, Dead On Arrival!
Tupac was a producer, singer/songwriter and a father, and will be
remembered by many people in many places for a long, long time to come.

Krystyna Scullion (14)

Information

We hope you have enjoyed reading this book - and that you will continue
to enjoy it in the coming years.

If you like reading and writing poems and stories drop us a line, or give us
a call, and we'll send you a free information pack.

**Write to: Young Writers Magazine and Competition Information,
Remus House, Coltsfoot Drive, Woodston,
Peterborough PE2 9JX
(01733) 890066**